How to Study the Bible for Beginners

Mastering the Art of Biblical Interpretation and Applying It to Your Life

Welcome Aboard, Check Out This Limited-Time Free Bonus!

Ahoy, reader! Welcome to the Ahoy Publications family, and thanks for snagging a copy of this book! Since you've chosen to join us on this journey, we'd like to offer you something special.

Check out the link below for a FREE e-book filled with delightful facts about American History.

But that's not all - you'll also have access to our exclusive email list with even more free e-books and insider knowledge. Well, what are ye waiting for? Click the link below to join and set sail toward exciting adventures in American History.

Access your bonus here
https://ahoypublications.com/
Or, Scan the QR code!

Table of Contents

Introduction

This book is the start of a great new you!

It is your journey toward a deeper spiritual life through understanding and connection with your Bible. "How to Study the Bible for Beginners: Mastering the Art of Biblical Interpretation and Applying It to Your Life" is not only another Bible study guide. It's designed specifically for you—the beginner, the seeker, the one who wants to make sense of this ancient and powerful text but is unsure where to start.

This book provides the tools, techniques, and insights to make your Bible study meaningful and practical. Whether you've just begun your walk with God or have been a Christian for years, this book aims to make Bible study accessible and engaging. You'll see the "how" and "why" of the events and teachings to help you build a strong foundation for lifelong learning and spiritual growth.

Its clear, conversational tone and step-by-step approach sets this guide apart. You won't find complex theological jargon or overwhelming academic discussions. Instead, you'll discover hands-on methods and practical instructions tailored to help you navigate and understand the Bible. Each chapter takes you deeper into your study, offering practical strategies to apply immediately.

There's so much to explore in this book's pages – for instance, the importance of a Bible study routine and developing one that works for you, the foundational principles of Bible interpretation, and learning to approach the scriptures with the right mindset and tools. You'll be guided through effective study tools and resources that will enrich your study sessions. You'll explore the Bible's historical and cultural contexts for a richer understanding of the text. This book reveals study themes within the Bible and how to recognize them for the bigger picture of God's message, so applying the scriptures to your daily living will become seamless. Lastly, you'll learn about the power of community Bible study and the value of shared learning and accountability.

This book is your companion on a journey of discovery and transformation. As you turn each page, you will become more confident and equipped to study the Bible more insightfully and transformatively. Discover how the Word of God can become a living, breathing part of your life.

Chapter 1: The Importance of Bible Study

It's easy to gloss over this chapter or skip it entirely because you already know why you want to study the Bible. After all, you wouldn't have bought this book or attempted to read it if you didn't have an idea of the importance of Bible study. However, you don't want to miss the foundation laid by the content embedded within this first chapter.

Learning how to study the Bible can be easy and exciting if you do it right.[1]

When the initial excitement wears off—and it happens to everyone—what will keep you going is a solid understanding of why Bible study matters. This chapter will help you solidify your Bible study foundation so you'll have the strength and motivation to stay on course, even on tough days. Tough days are when you do not feel like picking up your Bible, or you might consider mindlessly glossing over a chapter you intended to study. Recalling all the amazing benefits of a dedicated Bible study life will boost your morale and discipline to do what's right.

There is a need for intentional study of the Word of God if your life as a Christian must wax strong and grow. It's like what you eat to stay healthy—80% of the time, it's an activity you find pleasurable and enjoyable. You want to eat without being told and don't mind doing it multiple times daily. Consuming the Word of God should be the same. It's an activity that, as a Christian, you should love doing. However, unlike food, its importance goes beyond the physical benefits to helping you build your spirit.

This chapter explains how well the Word of God can influence and change your life. If you desire to know Jesus, this chapter will fuel it by giving you more reasons to validate your desire.

The Significance of Studying the Bible

An unending supply of self-help and motivational books is available that touch on various facets of human life and address essential issues people face daily. However, the one thing no book or author has accomplished is the Bible's all-encompassing nature. Despite being thousands of years old, the Bible's enduring relevance and ability to come alive for those who diligently seek its wisdom have sustained it for centuries past and will for centuries to come.

The Bible is a book covering all areas of life. A fitting name for this book could be "Life's Guide" or "The Living Manual," yet even these titles wouldn't fully encapsulate its contents, as its benefits span beyond the physical and extend to the eternal. The Bible guarantees the greatest honor, abundant riches, overflowing joy, unending peace, a long and well-lived life, and the greatest gift of all—eternal life. The Bible offers you the knowledge of a life with God.

Any book or material attempting to solve life's problems is merely an attempt based on personal experiences or those of others. A manual on how to fix a machine, if not written by the manufacturer, is nothing but a poor imitation. There's nothing like the original. Every other attempt won't be as good as the creator's work. God created this world. He provided the template for how it operates and how to live in it.

Therefore, the Bible is infused with His life force—the Holy Spirit.

As the scripture says:

"For prophecy never had its origin in the human will, but prophets, though human, spoke from God as they were carried along by the Holy Spirit" (2 Peter 1:21, NIV).

And:

"In the beginning was the Word, and the Word was with God, and the Word was God" (John 1:1, NIV).

Furthermore:

"All scripture is given by the inspiration of God..." (2 Timothy 3:16, NKJV).

These scriptures help explain that the Bible is no ordinary book. Although written on Earth by humans, it was divinely inspired by the Holy Spirit. Knowing that God's heart has been revealed to you should help you stay more focused on your studies. This consciousness will propel you forward in your journey.

Below are the benefits of studying the Bible, showing you the importance of Bible study and its many upsides:

A Personal Transformation

Before anything else, you must first be transformed. Every change in your life starts from within. Transformation begins when you start studying the Bible intentionally. The Bible is a light in this dark world, teaching you what to do and helping you become a better person.

The Bible will allow you to find inner peace and happiness.'

"Thy Word is a lamp unto my feet and a light unto my path.
"(Psalms 119:105, NIV).

Character flaws that you are aware of and those hidden block you from shining as a light in the world and being a blessing to those around you are revealed and purged when you intentionally study the word of God. Human traits, such as lying, stealing, selfishness, self-centeredness, backbiting, gossiping, laziness, procrastination, masturbation, pornography, murmuring, complaining, grumbling, envy, anger, aggression, malice, hatred, and many others rise to the surface to be purged. The Word of God makes you conscious of these flaws, strengthens you to grow above them, and not be easily swayed by them.

It's like winnowing, where grains get sifted to separate the valuable from the impurities. Studying the Bible helps you sift through your character flaws. By bringing these flaws to the surface, you can address and remove them, allowing your true, refined self to emerge.

Like gold going through the fire, a Bible study will do the same for you. Gold must endure the intense heat of a furnace to be purified—removing impurities and dross—so will your character as a Christian undergo a refining process through studying the scriptures. When gold gets subjected to fire, it melts, and the impurities rise to the surface and get skimmed away. Similarly, as you delve into the Bible, the heat of spiritual examination and reflection exposes the imperfections and flaws within you. This intense scrutiny allows you to confront and address these imperfections, leading to growth and spiritual maturity. The Word of God acts as the divine fire, purifying your heart and mind, refining your character, and strengthening your faith like the fire refines gold.

There's the story of a lady who served under a kind woman. Although treated with the utmost kindness, she grumbled and complained about everything. She had grown accustomed to complaining about every little thing in her life. She had no reason to be joyful, as her grumblings had clouded everything, she could be grateful for. One day, when her boss was not around, she came across a verse in the Bible during her study time:

"Do everything without grumbling or arguing, so that you may become blameless and pure, children of God without fault in a warped and crooked generation" (Philippians 2:14-15, NIV).

Seeing this for the first time, she felt like she had been jolted out of a dream-like state. God's Word tenderly spoke of rebuke and conviction.

It strengthened her resolve to change and do better. Immediately, she repented and humbled herself before God, apologized to her boss when she returned, and made amends with others to whom she may have acted ungratefully. From that day, she changed her ways and loved herself more.

There are many stories of individuals whose habits and characters changed for the better by studying God's Word. It doesn't happen overnight. However, you will experience true personal transformation by giving yourself wholeheartedly to studying. The Word of God leaves no stone unturned.

Enhanced Wisdom

This is another exceptional benefit and importance of studying the Bible. The Bible says,

"For the LORD gives wisdom; from his mouth comes knowledge and understanding" (Proverbs 2:6 NIV)

also, the psalmist in Psalms 119:144 (NIV) says,

"... give me understanding that I may live."

Wisdom is crucial in navigating life. However, God's wisdom is not the wisdom of this world, as Apostle Paul clearly distinguishes in 1 Cor. 1:20 and 3:19. You need the wisdom from God to live a victorious life. You can find this wisdom embedded in His Word. All through the Bible, the writers in the Old and New Testament books wrote about how vital having wisdom is and how detrimental it would be to live without it. The psalmist regards it as life itself.

There are no limitations to God's wisdom. His wisdom can appear or be appropriate anywhere - academics, business, family, relationships, etc. God's wisdom makes provision for every aspect of life. The Bible states that once, during Moses' time, God singled out a man, Bezalel, and gave him wisdom to be an expert craftsman and artisan.

"Then the Lord said to Moses, See, I have chosen Bezalel son of Uri, the son of Hur, of the tribe of Judah, and I have filled him with the Spirit of God, with wisdom, with understanding, with knowledge and with all kinds of skills to make artistic designs for work in gold, silver, and bronze, to cut and set stones, to work in wood, and to engage in all kinds of crafts." (Exo 31:1-5 NIV)

Also, in Psalms 119, the psalmist talks about how God's wisdom from His Word gave him an edge and helped him excel.

"By considering your commands I have an edge over my enemies, for I take seriously everything you say. You have given me more understanding than those who teach me, for I've absorbed your eye-opening revelation. You have graced me with more insight than the old sages because I have not failed to walk in the light of your ways." (Psalms 119:98-100 TPT)

When God's Word enters your heart, it becomes wisdom, shining a light on the directions through life. The Bible says that when God's Word comes and enters your heart, you receive not only understanding but also light.

"The entrance of Your word gives light; it gives understanding to the simple." (Psalm 119:130 NKJV)

An elderly woman lived in Kentucky and was known for her deep knowledge and sound judgment. Although she never received a formal education and had spent most of her life tending to her modest home and garden, she was full of wisdom. Many people sought to speak with her, and all who encountered her left enlightened and uplifted. Everyone, including her neighbor, fellow farmers, merchants, and the town's mayor, often sought her counsel.

Intrigued by her wisdom, a visitor asked her how she possessed such knowledge. She smiled warmly and replied that her only secret was a lifetime of studying the Bible and praying. She told him that before the sun rose every morning, she would sit by her window with her Bible in hand, meditating on the scriptures. "The Bible," she said, "Is a well that never runs dry. Every time I open its pages, I draw up a little more wisdom to guide me through the day."

Now, imagine how much more impact you can have on Christ by storing His sound wisdom in you.

A Deeper Understanding of Life's Purpose

An in-depth study of God's Word reveals the true purpose for which you were created on this Earth. With all its chaos and never-ending activities in life, it's easy to lose sight of what is important and go with the flow of what everyone else does. However, studying God's Word calms the other voices and every noise, giving you clarity on your purpose.

An in-depth study of the Bible will give you revelations about your life's purpose.[3]

Many people base their life choices on family and peers' opinions, especially during the early stages of life. Later, they become bothered and troubled, resulting in one of the most asked questions: "Why am I even here?" Many have this question constantly stuck in their hearts, and they keep searching for the answer. That answer comes to everyone only from the Word of God.

William Wilberforce, a well-known British politician and philanthropist is a great example of someone who discovered his true purpose through studying God's Word. During his early years, he lived a comfortable life, enjoying the luxuries and social circles resulting from his status. Although raised with Christian values, his faith didn't touch his daily life. He often felt lost, drifting through life without a clear direction. Everything changed in his mid-twenties. He experienced a profound spiritual awakening when he began studying the Bible intentionally. It completely transformed his outlook on life. The more he read and prayed, the more he understood God's unique purpose for him—something far more significant than success or approval from others.

As he immersed himself in the scriptures, it became clear to him that his calling was to fight for the abolition of the slave trade in Britain. It was no easy task as he faced enormous opposition and challenges. However, Wilberforce remained steadfast and deeply convinced that

God's assignment was for him to stand up for the dignity and freedom of every human. His connection to God's Word gave him the clarity, strength, and courage to pursue this mission, even when the odds were against him.

Wilberforce's journey shows how studying God's Word can clarify your life and help you discover your true purpose. When you quieten the noise around you and focus on God's voice through the scriptures, you find answers to your deepest questions and the courage to follow His path.

Potential Challenges One Might Face in the Study of the Bible

No challenge is insurmountable. So long as you decide in your heart to intentionally study God's Word, it is backed up by God's grace, helping you with the journey. Your journey will have lapses and drawbacks, but if you return to the right path, you will reach your desired end.

A few challenges to expect are:

Finding Time for Study

Finding the right time to study is not always easy. Fixing a set time is the ideal, as it helps you keep to a schedule. Most people choose the early morning hours or before retiring to bed or both, but your schedule shouldn't be cast in stone. However, it is good for its many benefits, like little to no distractions, a clear mind, etc., and any time will work. You must find what time works best so that you can stick to it and not be interrupted by anything else.

Also, while trying to stick to your selected study time, go for the next best thing if you can't make it work some days. Perhaps read on the go as Bibles and study guides are readily available on phones, tablets, and other gadgets in text and audio format. It may not be the same as studying at your fixed time, but it will help to supplement lapses and help you stay true to your study.

Feelings of Discouragement

Another frequently experienced challenge in studying the Bible is discouragement. Many people get discouraged for different reasons, including family, friends, work, academics, etc. Some might feel discouraged when they're unable to understand and fully comprehend complex passages. Therefore, it's good to have friends, groups, or someone with a higher knowledge of the faith to whom you can reach out for help. You will have improved your understanding and interpretation of God's Word.

Experiencing these challenges is normal for a Christian navigating life. The only secret is not to allow them to hold up your journey. What seemed like an enormous task will soon become easy with persistence and patience. You can do this!

Long-Term Benefits of Consistent Bible Study

Here are three long-term benefits:

Strengthened Faith

You can't pray your way into faith or a strong faith. Your faith is greatly increased and strengthened as you study the Bible continuously. It's only by studying the Word of God that your faith grows. The Bible says:

"Faith cometh by hearing, and hearing by the word of God"
(Rom. 10:17)

A minister gained an understanding from an experience based on this scripture. At a time, he constantly prayed for faith, asking God to give him great faith, and he prayed earnestly. He did this for a while, but nothing happened. One day, he stumbled upon the above scripture. He realized he wouldn't be imbued with great faith by desiring and praying about it but only through a dedicated study of God's Word.

When you read God's Word, it comes alive in your heart, and the Holy Spirit ministers to you. Hearing the written word from your Bible brings faith, and the Bible impacts many of the benefits of great faith.

Improved Decision Making

Another long-term benefit of studying your Bible is the wisdom gained from it. Once you study your Bible dedicatedly, you will watch your choices evolve and become more informed. You'll become more inclined to make the right decision even if all the facts are unconfirmed because you act by the wisdom of God's Word.

Greater Inner Peace

The third benefit of a long-term study of God's Word is the profound word PEACE. This singular word is what everyone wants. A desire to be at peace layers the walls of the human heart – and only God can guarantee this peace. The Bible says,

"You will keep him in perfect peace, whose mind stays on You because he trusts in You." (Isa 26:3 NKJV)

Also,

"Peace I leave with you; my peace I give you. I do not give to you as the world gives. Do not let your hearts be troubled and do not be afraid." (John 14:27 NIV)

These scriptures reveal God's desire to give all His children peace and how to get it. Without a study of God's Word, it will be impossible to know what He has said about His peace and how you can free yourself of your troubles, worries, and cares.

The importance of Bible study time cannot be overstressed. The word of God is needed to grow and live a blessed life. To know that Word, you must study the Bible. So, get studying. A victorious life awaits you!

End-of-Chapter Checklist

Here are a few items you need to tick off if you have them to help your Bible study journey:

- ☐ A Bible
- ☐ Translations
- ☐ A Journal
- ☐ A quiet study space

Chapter 2: Different Bible Translations and What They Mean

They say variety is the spice of life, which is also true for the many translations of the Bible available. Each translation is known for its particular style and perspective. However, the ultimate aim is the same – to convey the Word of God – translations as different routes bring you to the same destination. Each path gives a different view, but the endpoint is a more profound revelation of Jesus Christ. So, whether you take a more direct route, a literal one, poetic or expressive, each translation aims to ensure you understand and connect with the heart of scriptures – God's Word.

It's a good idea to explore different translations to be able to gain different perspectives and a deeper understanding of the scriptures.'

These readily available translations give you a look into the scriptures to view the wisdom in the Word of God. There's always something in these translations that will meet your particular needs, preferences, or understanding. When you use a translation, Bible study, which can be daunting, even to the seemingly seasoned Christian, becomes an enjoyable and approachable experience.

As a Christian, the Bible is a crucial and vital component of your faith, containing God's intentions, thoughts, and laid-out plans. As a book holding vital information, it cannot afford to have its message miscommunicated or misunderstood. So, this chapter will help you understand the various translations and how the Word of God is communicated. It covers everything you need to make an informed choice. So, buckle up and dive in!

The Reason for the Existence of Multiple Bible Translations

Multiple translations of the Bible haven't always existed. When first compiled, it was written in three primary languages: Hebrew, Aramaic, and Greek. It is common knowledge that the Old Testament was written in Hebrew. However, what is not well known is that a small section was also written in Aramaic. Greek was the only language accepted by the Southern Mediterranean people at that period. For centuries, anyone interested in studying the Bible had to read in that language. This privilege was reserved for the aristocrats and those considered "high borns," limiting access to the Word of God and restraining its propagation and advancement. To common people, their only access to the Bible was what they were taught from the scriptures by those who could read.

As Christianity spread rapidly across many regions, the need to make the Bible accessible to more people became a pressing demand. The Septuagint, a translation of the Old Testament from Hebrew to Greek, was the first step toward the many translations to follow. Afterward, Saint Jerome translated the Latin Vulgate. However, these efforts count as a chip in the tree since these translations were only accessible to the educated elite, who could read Greek and Latin.

A ray of light on the quest for Bible translation only came in the 15th century with the arrival of the printing press. Individuals like John Wycliffe and Martin Luther pioneered this development and translated the Bible into a more familiar language for the people. The former wrote a Middle English version, and the latter translated it into Saxon German. However, this task was not without its challenges for the pioneers. They encountered much opposition to their work, but their persistence paved the way for others to follow. It's hard to describe just how revolutionary their actions were. They were more than linguistic translations and printing the Word. They were instrumental in God's will being accomplished. They gave ordinary people access to the scripture in languages they understood.

Sir Wycliffe and Martin Luther's efforts were profound. Due to the rapid changes and evolution in languages, it was clear that translations were needed. Although monumental in its time, the King James Version was not sufficient for the growth and spread of Christianity. New, modern translations emerged, each with the same aim – to bridge the gap between today's readers and the ancient text. These new translations wanted to improve the text's readability and its authenticity. For this reason, this new, modern translation bears the banner of the effort by the scholars of old, who poured their lives out for the advancement of the Bible while preserving the integrity of the Word, regardless of the times.

Ultimately, despite their differences, all the translations point to the same foundational truth—to reach the same end—a clearer understanding of God's Word and a closer relationship with Jesus Christ.

The Different Translations

More than 200 versions of the Bible exist in over 70 languages. With this many translations in circulation, it's unsurprising that several Christians have issues finding what works without getting confused. There are several known ways of categorizing the translations of the Bible. This chapter covers the most well-known ones. Below is a list of the translations divided into sections, each with popular examples and what makes them different from the other. When categorizing different Bible translations, you can use several approaches to organize them effectively:

By Target Audience

- **Scholarly/Academic:** This translation is for in-depth study and precision (e.g., NRSV, NET).

- **Devotional/General Reading:** This translation aims at everyday readers and devotionals (e.g., NIV, NLT).

- **Children/Young Adults:** As the name implies, it's adapted and better suited for younger audiences (e.g., International Children's Bible).

By Denominational Preference

- **Protestant Translations:** Primarily for the people within this denomination. (e.g., KJV, NKJV).

- **Catholic Translations:** This includes books accepted in the Catholic canon (e.g., NABRE, Douay-Rheims).

- **Orthodox Translations:** For Orthodox traditions (e.g., Orthodox Study Bible).

By Language and Regional Variations

- **English Translations:** Various English versions (e.g., KJV, NIV, ESV).

- **Translations in Other Languages:** Versions in other languages (e.g., Spanish Reina-Valera, French Louis Segond).

By Historical Development

- **Historical Editions:** Early translations and versions (e.g., Septuagint, Vulgate).

- **Modern Translations:** Contemporary versions (e.g., NLT, CSB).

By Translation Philosophy

This is the most common way to categorize Bible translations. This translation style aims to help Christians understand the primary focus of each translation. It could be to preserve the original Word in the first version or to make the text more readable, relatable, and understandable. Here are the sections in this category:

- **Formal Equivalence:** Known as "word-for-word" translation. The Bible translations in this section aim to stay close to the original text. Most of the original version's words and structure have not been altered. Examples include the New American Standard Bible (NASB) and the English Standard Version (ESV).

  "...through whom we have received grace and apostleship to bring about the obedience of faith for the sake of his name among all the nations..." (Rom 1:5)

- **Dynamic Equivalence**: Also called "thought-for-thought" translation. This translation aims to convey the meaning and intent of the original text for easy understanding. Examples include the New International Version (NIV) and the New Living Translation (NLT).

  "Through Christ, God has given us the privilege and authority as apostles to tell Gentiles everywhere what God has done for them, so that they will believe and obey him, bringing glory to his name." (Rom 1:5)

- **Paraphrase:** The translations in this section are the most recent attempts at using a contemporary writing style. They aim for a reader-friendly and easy-to-understand text. These translations go for clarity rather than strict accuracy. Examples include The Message (MSG) and The Living Bible (TLB).

  "...Through him, we received both the generous gift of his life and the urgent task of passing it on to others who receive it by entering into obedient trust in Jesus." (Rom 1:5)

- **Optimal Equivalence:** This translation balances formal and dynamic approaches. Instead of picking a side, they provide a balance between accuracy and readability. Examples are the Christian Standard Bible (CSB), the New Revised Standard Version (NRSV), and, more recently, The Passion Bible (TPT).

  "...Through him grace cascaded into us, empowering us with the gift of apostleship, so that we can win people from every nation into the obedience that comes from faith, to bring honor to his name." (Rom 1:5)

The Significance of Accuracy and Readability in Bible Translations

The text's readability and accuracy are vital when considering a Bible translation. Accuracy ensures the translation stays true, maintaining the core message and the original text's intent is intact. The Bible has divine authority because efforts were made to adhere faithfully to the original text's context. This cannot be compromised because it makes the Bible a reliable guide for spiritual growth and understanding. Without accuracy, a translation risks distorting God's Word, which could lead to misunderstandings or misinterpretations of essential truths within the Bible.

However, readability is as important. When a text is accurate, but comprehension becomes challenging, it becomes a problem because the text's value reduces. Beyond words, the Bible is a living document that comes alive within you, speaking to your heart and mind. Once this text becomes complex, successful communication of the message to you, the reader, becomes distorted. If you can't read the Bible, you can't access its message. If you can't access its message, you can't understand it. If you can't understand it, you can't engage with God's Word meaningfully, regardless of your reason for studying.

So, these factors are crucial because they ensure the heart of the message is received. Perhaps, due to words, structure, or both changing, the result could be misinformation. Also, a lack of readability will prevent you from comprehending or understanding the message, defeating the study's purpose. The balance of these factors – accuracy and readability – is the key to finding a Bible translation that works for you. A translation that is faithful to the original scriptures and easy to understand helps ensure that God's Word will guide you in your faith journey. Hence, the Bible becomes a reliable and approachable source of spiritual nourishment, helping you grow closer to God and understand His will.

Practical Advice on Selecting a Suitable Bible Translation Based on Personal Study Goals and Preference

Choosing the right Bible translation depends on your goal for Bible study. With so many translations available, finding one that meets your needs, whether seeking deep theological insight, easy readability, or a balance of both, is essential. When choosing your preferred Bible translation, consider the following:

Consider Your Study Goals

When studying the Bible, if you aim to get deeper theological insight, translations like the New American Standard Bible (NASB) or the English Standard Version (ESV), which pay closer attention to accuracy, might be the best choice. These translations stay as close to the original text as possible, making them ideal for an in-depth study. On the other hand, if your interests lie in devotional reading and everyday casual study, opt for translations like the New Living Translation (NLT) or the New International Version (NIV), which give more clarity and readability.

Match the Translation to Your Reading Style

If you learn you are more of a modern language go-to individual who loves and prefers relatable expressions, consider translations like the Message (MSG) or the New Living Translation (NLT). These translations are often written in a more conversational tone, unlike translations such as the King James Version (KJV) or the New King James Version (NKJV), which will be better suited if you prefer the traditional style. They bring a historical richness rather than the engaging approach of the former.

Consult Study Aids

Study aids are another consideration in your Bible translation choice. Examples like cross-references, footnotes, and study guides provided within a translation make them a good choice for an excellent Bible study experience.

Experiment and Compare

Another good way to enrich your Bible study is by experimenting and comparing Bible translations. Each translation has something new and fresh, whether it's a change in wording, cultural contact, or writing style. When you compare, you get a broader view of the message, deepening your understanding. Sometimes, when you read a passage, it may seem difficult in one translation. However, if you look at it from another, it becomes clearer. You will see how they tackled its difficulty and simplified it for easy understanding. Studying this way simplifies the text's meaning and enlightens key insights you may have missed in your first read. The translator's beliefs and language choices often shape these translations, so make sure you don't get caught in the web of a single translation bias. Multiple options give you a rounded view.

Making notes and exploring comparisons is encouraged.[5]

Multiple translations give you a fresh view of the text, ensuring your study is fresh and engaging. A text you have previously read could take on a new significance because you read it in a different translation. The Holy Spirit will help you receive light from the same passage in that moment.

Additionally, certain translations might resonate more with you when memorizing or applying scripture, making them easier to remember or live by. Lastly, multiple translations can help you communicate more effectively if you teach or share the Bible with others. If your audience needs a simpler, more accessible version, there's a provision available. If they seek one more theologically precise, there's a provision available. Multiple translations allow you to tailor your message to meet their needs better.

Using multiple Bible translations is like viewing a diamond from different angles. Each perspective reveals new facets and depths of meaning. It enriches your understanding of scripture and strengthens your connection to its truths, making your study more dynamic, balanced, and spiritually fulfilling.

Seek God's Guidance

Ultimately, your Bible translation choice isn't only practical, like what shoe to wear. It's more profoundly personal and spiritual. As a Christian, you are not only an earthly person. It's apparent in the Bible that all who've been raised to live in Christ are spirit beings. When you choose a translation, take time and seek God's guidance through prayer. Ask Him to help you find a version that best supports your growth journey and strengthens your relationship with Him. Pray for clarity to understand how translations align with your spiritual needs and how they can enrich your study of His Word. Trust that with prayerful consideration, you'll choose a translation that resonates with your heart and enhances your walk with God.

How to Effectively Integrate Multiple Translations into Your Study and Not Get Confused

It's advisable to start with translations known for their accuracy to effectively use and incorporate multiple Bible translations in your study routine. These versions stick closer to the original text and will help you understand the core message. Once you get comfortable with these, you can move on to easier-to-read and understand translations.

Here's a simple way to do it:

Start with Accurate Translations: Begin by reading a verse or chapter in translations known for their close adherence to the original texts. This will help you precisely understand what the Bible says in that verse.

Switch to Readable Translations: Next, look at translations like the NLT, TPT, or even The Message translation. These are easier to read and can offer fresh insights or a clearer explanation of the text.

Take Notes: As you read, jot down your thoughts and understanding of each translation. Note differences or new insights.

Compare and Reflect: After reading the verse or chapter in different translations, compare your notes. See how each translation adds to your understanding and helps clarify the message.

Seek the Holy Spirit's Guidance: Never forget this part. Throughout this process, pray continually, asking the Holy Spirit to guide you. His insight will significantly help you piece together the whole meaning of the verse or passage and apply it to your life.

Following these steps, you will get the best of both worlds: a well-rounded view of the scripture and an increased depth of understanding, making studying more engaging and insightful. You won't often have to worry about getting confused while studying. However, if you get confused, do not let the words get to you. Instead, focus on the message's central core to settle concerns in your heart and bring the understanding home.

Bible Study Resources

Here's a list of resources you can use to compare Bible translations:

- **Bible Apps:** YouVersion, Olive Tree, Logos Bible Software, Blue Letter Bible, etc.
- **Parallel Bibles:** The NIV/NLT Parallel Bible, The ESV/ESV Study Bible, and The KJV/NKJV Parallel Bible.
- **Online Bible Comparison Tools:** Bible Gateway, Bible Hub, and StudyLight.
- **Printed Bible Comparison Books:** The New Strong's Exhaustive Concordance of the Bible and The Comparative Study Bible.
- **Bible Dictionaries and Study Guides:** The HarperCollins Bible Dictionary and The Zondervan NIV Study Bible.

Ultimately, the best Bible translation is the one you will read conveniently, helping you draw closer to God. Considering your study goals, reading preferences, and purpose, you will find a translation that meets your needs and enriches your spiritual journey. You Can Do This!

End-of-Chapter Checklist

Check this list to find your preferred Bible translation:

- ☐ Identify Your Needs
- ☐ Compare Translations
- ☐ Evaluate Study Aids
- ☐ Use Comparison Tools
- ☐ Consider Theological Perspective
- ☐ Check for Language and Style
- ☐ Seek Recommendations
- ☐ Test Different Translations
- ☐ Pray for Guidance
- ☐ Make Your Choice

Chapter 3: Developing a Personal Bible Study Routine

Here's a quick game to prepare you for this chapter. You need to answer Yes, No, or Maybe to the following questions:

1. Do you struggle to maintain a regular Bible study?
2. Do you feel overwhelmed when you sit down to study?
3. Do you often drift off to sleep during your study time?
4. Do distractions easily pull you away from your Bible study?
5. Do you have difficulty staying focused for extended periods?
6. Do you struggle to stick to a consistent study schedule?

Take a moment to think about your answers.

Developing a Bible Study routine makes it easier to stay committed.[6]

Now that you've answered these questions, you might see a pattern in your Bible study challenges. Don't worry. You're not alone. Others have gone and are going through the same challenge. This shows there are tested and tried ways to develop a functional Bible study routine, which is the primary aim of this chapter. This chapter explores common hurdles, addresses them, and explains how overcoming them will help you develop a Bible study routine that fits your lifestyle and keeps you engaged. Discover how to turn your Bible study experience into a rewarding and integral part of your daily life.

The Benefits of a Regular Bible Study Routine

A lady shared the testimony of her Bible study journey on her blog. Her experience was indeed wonderful. Before successfully completing her intense one-year study, she often studied the Word of God in short bursts. Her Bible study was only during peculiar seasons. She identified the problem and looked for ways to tackle it. She found temporary relief in the things she loved – trying recommended study styles and tools and taking part in Bible challenges on popular Bible apps like YouVersion. However, these were quick fixes. Even the Bible challenge activities held occasionally at church were not enough to get her to where she wanted to be in her study of the Bible. It wasn't until she committed to reading the Bible in a year that her passion for the scriptures truly grew.

During this year, she was intentional about daily Bible reading and study. She ensured a day wouldn't go by without reading her Bible, even for 5 minutes.

Although she fumbled a few times, sometimes she missed weeks on her planned routine. Despite these fluctuations, perseverance made her story beautiful, like many others with similar stories. In a little over a year, she had completed her reading goal. It's easy to dwell on the fact that it wasn't precisely a year to read the entire Bible, but it was a year of Bible study for her. Her story is a testament to how a consistent routine, although sometimes flexible, can strengthen your dedication and determination to study the Bible and deepen your connection to God.

The benefits of a regular Bible study routine are numerous and worthwhile. Once you experience them, you will wonder why you have ever struggled. Here are a few benefits:

A Better Understanding

The most significant benefit of a regular Bible study routine is that it deepens your understanding of scripture. Studying the Bible as part of your day allows you to dig into the text. It broadens your mind and helps you understand the message clearly. When you read your Bible, it's like walking into a dark room with only a candle. You only see some parts but can't see the full view. The beauty is that you don't leave the room the same way you entered. The bits you uncover lighten more of the room, so when you re-enter, one candle at a time, you light up more areas, and your view gets clearer. Similarly, you develop a deeper understanding when you study God's Word.

When you make Bible study a regular part of your day, you familiarize yourself with God's Word, like getting to know a good friend – the more time you spend together, the better you understand them. The same goes for the Bible. You notice details you missed the previous day or see how a part connects with other parts of the Bible. Regular study helps you build a more complete picture of what the Bible says, not only on a surface level but in a way that makes its teachings more meaningful and relevant.

Moreover, as you develop this routine, you crave God's Word more. It becomes a part of your day, something you look forward to – a moment of peace and reflection you don't want to miss. Amazingly, this routine shifts from something you "have" to do to something you "want" to do.

A Strengthened Faith

Another great benefit is a strengthened faith. Understanding the Bible builds your faith and strengthens you as a Christian. Studying God's Word consistently and spending more time in His presence will shape your thoughts, words, actions, and heart. See it in the same light as a builder laying a building's foundations. The more he invests, the stronger and more unshakable the building will be.

This was clearly stated in the Bible when God, speaking to Joshua in the Book of Joshua 1:8, said,

"Keep this Book of the Law always on your lips; meditate on it day and night, so that you may be careful to do everything written in it. Then you will be prosperous and successful."
(Joshua 1:8)

Every time you dive into God's Word, you add a new brick to your faith foundation. Over time, this foundation becomes so strong it can support you through life's challenges. You trust God more, not because you know you should, but because you've seen His promises in the scriptures and watched them unfold in your life. Faith isn't only about believing. It's about you growing. Your understanding of God grows deeper with consistent Bible study, as does your trust in Him. So, a Bible study routine does much more for you than giving you information. It keeps you anchored. Why? It constantly reminds you of God's faithfulness, strengthens your belief, and encourages you to face whatever comes your way. The more you spend time in His Word, the stronger your faith becomes. That strength can carry you through anything.

Daily Spiritual Nourishment

Consistency in your study routine helps you understand the Bible better. It creates a healthy spiritual habit for daily nourishment. Soon, your day feels incomplete without it. Carving out a specific time for Bible study becomes a routine that will enrich the quality of your life and ensure you stay grounded in your faith. The more you stick to your routine, the more you'll want to go deeper, memorize, and truly live the scriptures you read.

How to Establish a Study Routine

Follow these steps to establish a study routine that works:

Setting a Consistent Study Schedule That Fits into Daily Life

As a Christian, a Bible study routine should be at the top of your activity list because it's transformative. The knowledge you learn goes beyond you, affecting others. Even knowing these benefits, many people still find it a challenge. You might start enthusiastically, but sustaining the momentum becomes the issue. Maybe you've previously set aside time for deep study, only to feel overwhelmed or get distracted. You might have tried to commit to a daily reading plan, but everyday life demands constantly pull you away. You are not alone. These are common issues many others have faced when establishing a consistent routine. However, many have proven it can be done. One way is creating a schedule for study time that fits into daily life. Don't be quick to say, "Well, I've been there, done that, and nothing has changed." The key to overcoming these challenges is simple but powerful: consistency. Like a task repeated over time becomes ingrained, so does a regular Bible study habit. If you review a subject for one hour every day over ten days, it's more likely to stick with you than if you force yourself for ten hours in a single day. This also applies to your spiritual growth. It's a popular philosophy that habits form within 21 days of daily practice, which also applies to your Bible study routine. The more consistently you engage with scripture, the more naturally it becomes a part of your daily life.

The question is, "How do I establish a consistent study routine?" Here are practical tips to help you achieve the consistency you desire:

• Start Small

Always begin with small, manageable steps. Think of it like planting a tiny seed. You don't expect a full-grown tree overnight, but you know it'll grow strong with time and care. So, the first thing is setting realistic goals. You might want to dive in for hours at a time when you start, but this enthusiasm can quickly lead to burnout. You can begin by committing 10, 15, or 20 minutes a day – it might not sound like much, but those minutes build consistency. Spending a little time daily in God's Word will do more for your spiritual growth than packing everything into one or two big sessions.

Starting small allows you to digest what you're reading. Instead of rushing through chapters, you can take your time, give yourself a minute to meditate on a verse or two, and let the meaning sink in. When you take this slower but thoughtful approach, scriptures go beyond letters and speak to you.

• Be Patient

Don't beat yourself up. Building a new habit takes time. It won't happen overnight. Days will come when it feels like a struggle to open your Bible. That's perfectly fine since the goal isn't perfection but progress. Being patient with yourself doesn't mean being laid back. Instead, you pick yourself up when you falter with renewed vigor to go harder. Remember, you're planting seeds in your heart each time you sit down to study, even if it's only for a few minutes. Over time, the seeds will take root, and your desire to spend time in the Word grows naturally.

• Aim for Manageable Sections

When you pick a book of the Bible to study, don't feel pressured into rushing through it all at once. Give yourself time to enjoy the journey. Focus on one book at a time. Although there are benefits to studying multiple books of the Bible at once, it's best to keep things simple as a beginner. The aim is to build a steady routine, so sticking with a single book will help you track your progress. This will, in turn, strengthen your consistency over time.

Another approach toward building a consistent Bible study routine is the thematic method. Focusing on themes can be an excellent method if you would rather learn from various books in a single go. Exploring specific themes within the Bible, such as Love, Faith, Joy, Forgiveness, Giving, Holiness, Salvation, etc., helps you trace how it appears across different Bible books and passages, so you get to see the broader picture of God's message. This method will enrich your understanding of each theme and keep your study time fresh and engaging as you navigate through the parts of the Bible while staying focused on a central topic.

Create a Distraction-Free Study Space

You should create your "Personal Sanctuary." Your go-to study space must be comfortable and free from distractions. A personal sanctuary is imperative for your Bible study's effectiveness. It will influence how much you enjoy your study time. This spot becomes your number one location from all the noise and clutter surrounding you. Here are a few ways to create a space to boost focus and reflection:

Create a study space that is free from distractions.'

- **Choose the Right Spot:**

When choosing a space, it must be right for you. A place that is quiet and where you can feel at peace. It could be a corner in your living room, a small nook in your bedroom, or a spot by your window. The important thing is to find peace and solace there.

- **Comfort Is Key:**

Your next thought should be comfort. You want to ensure your chosen study space is comfortable, not necessarily elaborate. A simple chair and table will do just fine. However, if you seek extra comfort, add a cushion, a throw blanket, and a pillow. The aim is to be comfortable and enjoy your study time, not to doze off. So, if you feel it too much, take it out.

- **Keep It Clutter-Free:**

You want a clean and clutter-free space. When your study space is organized, it will help clear your mind and reduce distractions. You only need the essentials in your space, such as your Bible, notebook, and other study materials. Remove unnecessary gadgets and your phone. Let others in your household know you have set aside a fixed time for Bible study so they can leave you alone.

- **Lighting Matters:**

Good lighting matters. Natural light is an ideal choice and advised. However, if that's unavailable, go for the next best thing. The idea is to make your choice of space as bright as possible. Choose a spot near a window, or when studying in the evening, get a lamp that is easy on your eyes. The proper lighting will help you stay alert and focused during your study time.

- **Personal Touches:**

This isn't necessary, but if you can, add a few items for personal touches, like your favorite scented candle, a plant, a frame you hold dear, etc. Anything to make your spot feel extra special. Little details will make it more personal and more spiritually enriching.

Making Use of Study Aids

Bible study tools, such as Journals, Bible apps, and devotionals, are another way of adding to your routine. These tools can be an extra pair of hands to help and support you on your spiritual journey, even though your journey is not hinged or dependent on them. They are like the icing on a cake or the cherry on the icing, an extra boost to help you stay engaged and focused.

Using study aids like journals, devotionals, and Bible apps can give your study sessions a 180-degree shift. For instance, if you use a journal, capture your thoughts, questions, and reflections as you read, making tracking your progress and understanding easier. A daily devotional provides structure and insights, offering bite-sized readings and applications. These are especially helpful on busy days when you might struggle to find time for study. Bible apps are another invaluable resource. They provide access to various translations, reading plans, and interactive tools on your phone or tablet.

Tips for Maintaining Consistency and Motivation

Even on days when you face challenges or have a hectic schedule, these tips will help you stay consistent:

- Set alarms and use reminders to alert and prompt you to start your study sessions on time.
- Track your progress to see how far you've come and keep you motivated.
- Ensure you remain flexible. Adjust your routine when needed to accommodate changes within your schedule.
- Involve others in your study routine. Consider joining a study group or sharing the insights you gained with your friends.
- Learn to celebrate the little achievements and milestones to help you stay motivated.
- Try to incorporate variety into your study routine using different methods and resources.
- Stay prayerful and seek spiritual guidance to strengthen your commitment.
- Remember, be patient with yourself. Building a consistent routine takes time.

What long-term benefits do you stand to enjoy when you consistently study your Bible? They are numerous. Consistency in studying God's Word impacts all aspects and quality of your life beyond what you can imagine. Over time, your decision-making skills and discernment improve, helping you navigate life's challenges with greater clarity and confidence. Another benefit is your faith grows as you engage regularly with God's Word, and your understanding and relationship with God deepens. Also, an unexplained comfort, reassurance, and spiritual grounding will accompany you through life.

End-of-Chapter Checklist

Check the box on things you've achieved.

☐ Identified a specific time each day for Bible study

☐ Designated a quiet, comfortable space free from distractions for your study sessions

☐ Bible translation and study tools aligning with your study goals

☐ Additional resources, like commentaries or Bible study guides if needed

☐ Set clear goals for what you want to achieve in your Bible study routine

Chapter 4: Learning the Basics of Bible Interpretation

Magret sat at her study table, feeling a wave of frustration while staring at Romans 10:17. "Does faith come by hearing the word of God, or does it come by hearing, and that hearing comes from the word of God?" she muttered to herself, unsure if her thoughts made sense. A verse that initially filled her with joy now confused her. She was eager to learn how to grow in faith but now felt stuck and unsure if she had interpreted the verse correctly. Should she take it literally or look for a deeper meaning she might have missed? It wasn't her first experience of uncertainty studying the Bible. She constantly struggled to grasp the true meaning of Bible passages and their message. However, this time, she was determined to understand.

There can be struggles when it comes to finding clarity, and this is why you need certain tools to work by.'

This frustration and confusion aren't something novel. Many can relate when studying the Bible. You get into God's Word with the best intentions, eager to learn and grow, only to become tangled in complex verses, which can be overwhelming and discouraging. Another worry for many is missing God's intention behind His words. Everyone wants to ensure they are not merely reading the Bible but truly understanding and applying it to their lives as God intended. So, when clarity becomes a problem, they feel lost or defeated in their spiritual journey.

This chapter will address these challenges on Bible interpretation basics and how to access tools to help you approach scripture confidently. You'll uncover how to connect with God's Word more profoundly, making your Bible study sessions more meaningful and enriching.

The Importance of Proper Interpretation

Jesus once said, *"I am the way, the truth, and the life..."* (John 14:6), and John accounted in John 1:1 that Jesus is the Word, as it says, *"...the Word was God."* So, if Jesus equals the Word, and Jesus equals Truth, then the Word is Truth. What then happens when people study the Bible and make interpretations based on personal experiences, temperaments, cultures, backgrounds, and personalities? Discrepancies creep in. The Bible's truth can get distorted and misunderstood because different people interpret it from individual experiences. So, it makes sense to try to get your interpretation right, avoid the pitfalls of personal bias, and stay anchored in the truth of God's Word. This truth communicates God's intentions for His words to prevent misunderstandings, help you grow in your faith, and better application to your life.

Key Principles of Interpretation

There are some guiding principles for better accuracy in interpreting the Bible. These principles must be understood and remembered for better accuracy. Here are the fundamental principles:

Context

Context explains the circumstances of a verse or passage in the Bible. It ensures you do not misinterpret a passage or isolate it from the intended meaning in the text. There are four categories of context to focus on for a better understanding of your study.

The first is the **"Immediate Context."** The texts immediately before and after the passage. For example, when reading a verse in the book of Philippians, consider its surrounding texts to fully grasp the issues discussed in the message delivered to the church at Phillipi. The context provides a snapshot of critical factors, like the specific situation, tone, and the passage's message. This helps eradicate misinterpretation based on a partial understanding of the complete message.

Next is the **"Broader context."** This goes beyond the preceding and proceeding text to the passage's broader context. For example, when studying a verse in Romans, you must decipher Paul's intent for his letter to the Romans and what role the verse or passage played in achieving it.

Another context is the **"Literary context."** The books of the Bible are rich in genres, such as narrative, poetry, prophecy, and epistles, each with its convention and purpose. Recognizing literary genres makes interpreting scriptures easier in light of their rhetorical and literary effects.

Last is the **"contextual consistency."**. Drawing an understanding from a verse or a whole passage must align with the Bible's message. Do not make interpretations outside the Bible's themes like Love, Grace, Redemption, etc.

An understanding of the various contexts determines how accurately you interpret the Bible. It helps to tackle the common mistake of isolating a verse or passage from their broader message.

Cross-Referencing

Cross-referencing is like a "comparison" because it means comparing related passages across parts of the scripture within the Bible. This method deepens your understanding and clarity of a passage by revealing its connection with other verses with similar themes or topics. When you compare two or more scriptures when studying a particular theme, you gain a broader perspective. For instance, consider branching out to other books or passages like James 2 and Romans 4 for a broader context and better understanding when studying faith in a book like Hebrews. Each passage observes or addresses the same thing from different standpoints. Approaching your study this way helps you understand the Bible's unified message. It safeguards you from misinterpretation or confusion. When you compare passages, you ensure your understanding stays within the Bible's overall message. Tools like concordances, topical guides, or Bible apps with cross-referencing features will streamline this process. They help enhance your study and simplify the connections of scriptures to improve your grasp of God's Word.

Understand the Original Audience

Another good way to see the thorough intent of a passage is by identifying its original audience. Each book of the Bible was written to and about specific people at particular times in history. Hence, each book has a different cultural, social, and historical context. When you know the original audience, you can better understand the intended meaning and application of the passage. For example, when reading Paul's letters to the Corinthians, knowing they were written to a church facing division and immorality issues helps you understand Paul's advice and corrections. Understanding this context reveals why certain instructions or teachings were given and how they addressed the needs and struggles of that community. This broadens your understanding and positions you to apply this ancient text better.

Interestingly, you don't have to research these yourself. Tools that have done the work are available. These tools unravel the historical background, cultural practices, and societal issues surrounding books and passages of the Bible. They include commentaries, history books, and biblical dictionaries.

When you consider these factors, you'll enjoy a more nuanced and accurate interpretation of the Bible.

The Significance of Considering Historical and Cultural Backgrounds

Imagine yourself at a family gathering (not your family) or in a group you've joined, where everyone communicates through inside jokes and references to past events. Not knowing their history or cultural context, keeping up becomes complicated, and you mostly feel lost. The jokes might seem confusing or even meaningless. This also applies to Bible study. Grasping the intended message of a passage necessitates understanding the text's historical and cultural background.

The Bible was written in various contexts thousands of years ago. Each context has its customs, beliefs, and societal norms. For example, consider Jesus's analogy about "sheep and shepherds"- at the time of His parables, shepherding in ancient Israel was a common and significant profession. Understanding the intricacies of shepherding will help you appreciate why Jesus uses this imagery to convey His themes about care, leadership, and guidance.

Shepherding relates to themes of leadership and guidance.[9]

Similarly, understanding the historical context of the early church will shed light on why certain issues in the New Testament were addressed. For example, Paul's letter in the book of Galatians addresses the confusion caused by those mixing Jewish law with the message of grace. Understanding the historical context here will help you understand the urgency and tone of Paul's corrections.

Cultural backgrounds hinged on factors like customs, traditions, and social norms of those times significantly influenced how the messages were received. For example, in ancient cultures, honor and shame were priorities. Knowing the weight they carried will help you understand the gravity of Paul's instructions about conduct in church and the community. Understanding this context reveals why certain positions, actions, or attitudes held much significance. Knowing about the Roman Empire's governance will explain the references to Roman officials and legal matters made in the New Testament.

Understanding the historical and cultural backgrounds of Biblical times enriches your study by giving you context that clarifies meanings better and deepens your understanding. This approach makes your study of the Bible more meaningful and relevant to your faith journey.

An Overview of Different Literary Genres in the Bible

A sound understanding of the Bible's literary genres also helps with accurate interpretation. The books of the Bible are written in various genres, each with the writer's characteristics and style, requiring you to approach them differently. Below is an overview of these genres:

Poetry

Psalms and Song of Solomon are good examples of books addressing themes poetically. They use vivid imagery, parallelism, and metaphor to convey deep emotional and spiritual truths. They express complex ideas and feelings through symbolic language and artistic expressions. For example, Psalms uses much parallelism, where thoughts are repeated or contrasted in successive lines, enhancing the lyrical quality and emphasizing the text's emotional depth. To interpret Biblical poetry effectively as a Christian, you must be aware of its symbolic nature and appreciate how the poetic devices contribute to the overall message.

Prophecy

This genre is present in books like Isaiah, Jeremiah, and Ezekiel. These books recorded prophetic declarations about God's will and future events by prophets who spoke on behalf of God. They delivered messages that carried immediate concerns and long-term visions. These books use symbolism and dramatic imagery that often make interpretation challenging. However, considering its surrounding contextual views, the interpretation becomes clearer. Prophetic texts are more than mere predictions. They call for repentance, justice, and faithfulness, which blends foretelling with forthtelling.

Narrative

The narrative genre is present in books like Genesis, Exodus, and the Gospels. These books convey theological truths by telling stories through historical events and personal experiences. This genre provides context and character development, like storytelling. It reveals how individuals and nations interacted with God, and their interpretation involves understanding the plot, character, motivations, and the broader message conveyed through the events. For instance, the story of Joseph in Genesis illustrates themes of providence and redemption through narratives from his trials and ultimate triumph.

Epistles

This genre is also called "letters" and appears in the New Testament, especially in the books written by the Apostle Paul. He wrote letters to churches and individuals on theological instruction and practical advice. These epistles addressed specific communities or individuals with particular issues and provided insights into early Christian beliefs and practices. When you read these letters, consider the historical situation and context in which they were written.

Epistles are also referred to as letters and address specific issues.[10]

Each genre in the Bible influences how its messages are shared and understood. Poetry, which uses symbolic language and emotional depth, requires you to appreciate its symbolic meanings. Prophecy needs you to interpret its historical context and symbolic elements to grasp its intended message fully. The narrative genre focuses on stories and deeper theological meanings, while epistles require understanding specific situations the doctrinal teachings address. Understanding and recognizing different forms enable the right approach when interpreting the Bible for a more precise understanding and application of its teachings.

Practical Steps for Interpreting Passages

Follow these steps for a straightforward interpretation of the Bible:

Read Entire Chapters or Books for Context

It's best to read an entire chapter or book to get the message of a passage or verse. When reading a verse, including the surrounding verses and the main context will help you see the bigger picture. When you understand how a specific verse fits into the overall story or message, you can avoid misunderstandings when reading a verse out of context. For example, knowing the overall message of the Book of James can help make sense of what it says about faith and good deeds.

Use Multiple Translations for Comparison

Reading several Bible translations can give you new insights and help clarify tricky passages. Compare translations to see how they interpret the same verse and note their differences. For example, suppose you look at a verse or passage from the King James Version and another translation, like the New International Version. In that case, you will notice a slight change in word choice and phrase, influencing your understanding.

Consider the Original Languages

Research the original Hebrew, Aramaic, or Greek words used in the passages. It could reveal the depth of the words that might have been lost in translation. You can use Bible study resources like original language tools or lexicons to help get the meanings and connotations behind these key terms. For example, consider the Greek word "agape," translated as "love." It has a specific connotation that differs from the English translation, revealing a deeper meaning that influences how you interpret passages on love.

Identify Literary Devices and Figures of Speech

Recognize and understand the literary devices used throughout the Bible, like similes, metaphors, and hyperboles. They help to convey profound truth more expressively. For example, Jesus often used parables – simple stories with deep moral or spiritual lessons when illustrating complex concepts.

Seek Different Points of View from Bible Study Groups

Discussing passages with others will elicit diverse perspectives and interpretations. Engaging in group discussions gives you a collaborative approach to understanding scripture. It highlights aspects of scriptures you might not have considered.

Pray for Guidance

Pray for insight and understanding before beginning your study. Seeking divine guidance helps you better grasp the text's spiritual truths and apply them to your life.

Consulting Commentaries and Study Guides

Encountering tough and challenging passages or unfamiliar contexts during Bible study is not strange. An excellent way to get a proper interpretation is through commentaries and study guides. These commentaries explain each verse, highlight insights from the original words, and reveal the passage's context. For example, a commentary on the book of Genesis clarifies the significance of ancient Near Eastern customs, which deepens your understanding of the text. Study guides are structured to lead you through specific books or themes in the Bible.

The only proper interpretation of God's Word is given by His Spirit according to 1 Cor 2:11. Everything mentioned in this chapter is a guide. Use them side-by-side as you seek inspiration and understanding from the Holy Spirit, and you shouldn't have any difficulty hearing and receiving God's clear message for you.

End-of-Chapter Checklist

Pick a verse of interest and follow the steps below to review its interpretation. Checking the boxes as you go forward:

☐ Consider the broader context.

☐ Cross-reference related passages.

☐ Use study tools like commentaries and study guides.

☐ Compare various Bible translations.

☐ Understand the original audience.

☐ Reflect on historical and cultural backgrounds.

☐ Evaluate different theological interpretations.

☐ Reflect on personal application.

Chapter 5: Utilizing Effective Study Tools and Resources

This chapter guides you through the practical aspect of Bible study – how to use various tools for a more effective and rewarding study time. Having these tools at your disposal is not enough, but understanding how to use them to enhance your connection with God's Word is helpful. Imagine how frustrating it is to build something without the proper tools. The same applies to the Bible. Without the right resources, it's easy to feel overwhelmed or stuck, especially when encountering passages. This chapter equips you with tools to understand challenging verses confidently during your study.

Using various tools while studying the Bible will help you create a more comprehensive picture of its meanings.[11]

As you learn the tools' functions, you'll discover new perspectives and better understand the Bible. Whether new to Bible study, budding, or knowledgeable, there's always something more to learn and explore. This chapter guides you on incorporating these resources into your study sessions, making your time with the Bible more structured, insightful, and impactful.

The Value of Using Study Tools in Bible Study

Using study tools while reading the Bible makes all the difference. The value and benefits are numerous. In this section, you'll learn four values:

• Gaining Deeper Knowledge

Consider these tools like crucial holders to keep your keys in place. They are not the actual keys, and you can do without them, but they save you the stress of searching for your keys. As you study the Bible, you'll encounter scriptures that seem straightforward at first. However, when you dig a little deeper, you'll be amazed at their profound meaning. Tools like study Bibles and commentaries help deepen your knowledge for greater understanding. They go beyond analyzing historical background knowledge and context to revealing more meaningful interpretations of verses. When you analyze a verse on "love" using these tools, you'll learn the word's origin, what it represents, and what it meant in ancient times. This way, the verse or passage is more significant and relatable. These tools allow you to explore God's Word, grow, improve your faith, and facilitate your relationship with God.

• Clarifying Complex Passages

The Bible can be challenging to understand, especially with complex or seemingly contradictory passages. However, there's so much beauty to find once you get the hang of better ways to study, using study tools and the help of the Holy Spirit. Study tools like concordance will help you trace where a specific word was used in other Bible verses to help you compare and contrast their usage for better clarity. Commentaries also help when you get stuck on a challenging verse. They help with scholarly explanations of Biblical verses and passages. These tools help you transform a moment of confusion into fresh learning.

• Building a Stronger Foundation for Faith

Another beauty of study tools is how they can help you strengthen your faith. The more you understand the Bible, the more confident you become in your belief. Using study tools regularly gives you the knowledge to grow in your faith and prepares you to share your beliefs with others. Study tools help solidify your knowledge, making your faith more resilient and your spiritual life more grounded.

• **Enriching the Overall Study Experience**

Besides amplifying your understanding of the Bible, study tools make your experience engaging and rewarding. Imagine reading a passage of the Bible, then turning to a map to see exactly where those events took place, and making fascinating discoveries like present-day Turkey, which is the Ephesus Paul spoke of, and Rome, which is today's Italy. Also, use a Bible dictionary to learn more about a specific term or concept.

These aids can transform your routine reading session from a regular to an interactive experience – and you'll not merely be absorbing information but actively exploring and discovering new things. It's like turning a black-and-white picture into color. The more you use these tools, the more vivid and alive the Bible becomes. This study enrichment experience keeps you motivated and excited to keep returning. There's always something new to uncover if you have the right tools.

The Various Types of Study Tools

By now, you should have an idea about these tools and resources. They are listed below for better comprehension and with more details on how they can practically enhance your Bible study experience.

Study Bibles

A study Bible is more than a regular Bible. It's a treasure chest containing additional resources for your spiritual enlightenment. A study Bible comprises commentary notes, cross-references, maps, and articles alongside the scripture. Picture when you read a book of the Bible, maybe Romans, and you came across a challenging passage about faith. If you had a study Bible instead of a regular one, the notes in your study Bible would have provided historical context, explained complex concepts, and suggested how a passage fitted into the larger message of the Bible. For example, a study Bible explains the cultural significance of Paul's writings to the Romans, helping you understand why his messages were considered so radical then. The cross-references would guide you to the other parts of the Bible relating to the verse, allowing you to decipher how parts of the Bible connect. The interconnected approach of a study Bible helps you build a more detailed understanding of Biblical themes and messages.

Commentaries

Commentaries are like having a Bible scholar sitting beside you, explaining the text as you read. You can relate to moments in school when you had someone by your side, a private tutor, friend, teacher, siblings, or parents, explaining the difficult part of a subject. Or when you faced a challenge that seemed so difficult at first, but when someone stepped in, it became so plain. See commentaries in the same light. However, a clear explanation is written instead of someone sitting beside you.

Commentaries are detailed books that give you a verse-by-verse analysis and interpretation of the scriptures. For instance, when studying the Book of Genesis, you become puzzled by the significance of God's covenant with Abraham. A good commentary breaks down the text, explains the original Hebrew terms, provides historical background, and discusses various interpretations from other scholars. This depth makes them particularly useful. They don't skim the surface but dive deeply into the text's intricate details. They explain common cultural and religious practices in those times to help you understand why events or commands were essential. Commentaries often discuss theological implications affecting your Christian faith. Consulting a commentary gives you a much richer and more detailed understanding of the Bible.

Concordances

Think of a concordance as a Biblical search engine helping you find specific verses or passages in the Bible. This tool lists words alphabetically and shows where each word appears in the Bible. For example, if you're studying faith, you can look up the word in a concordance and find every instance where faith appears throughout the Bible.

A concordance is very helpful during topical studies because it helps you gather all the verses of your study theme and will compare their development across the books of the Bible. Concordances help to bring clarity when the same words appear in different contexts by giving the word's meaning so you can see how it's applied in every context. For example, "love" is used in various ways, each with a slightly different meaning depending on the context.

Bible Dictionaries

They are considered the *Wikipedia* of the Christian faith or a Christian's guide for Biblical terms. For instance, if you come across the word "Pharisee" and have no idea what it means or who they were (or need a more in-depth understanding of their role and position), a Bible dictionary can help you. The dictionary shows the significance of terms, the cultural and historical background of each word, and their relevance in the Bible. You can quickly and easily fill gaps in your knowledge with a Bible dictionary, making your study time twice as productive.

Online Resources

The world is reveling in its digital living- everything revolves around the tech we use, even the Bible. Although a physical Bible is still encouraged, online tools for Bible study have many advantages. Many apps and websites are available on your phones and other devices for your Bible study. They provide multiple Bible translations, dictionaries, concordances, and commentaries at the tap of a screen. You can access these and more with a single app on your gadget instead of carrying large books. Apps like the BibleGateway or Blue Letter Bible enable you to compare translations, making it easier to grasp the text's message. Additionally, these online resources often have interactive features like word studies, cross-references, and audio commentaries to enhance your understanding further. The beauty is that most apps are free or cost little, making them accessible to everyone.

Using reliable online resources is a good way to find a variety of tools.[13]

Each study tool goes a long way in influencing your Bible study experience. Whether you want to decipher a complex passage, explore a specific theme, or understand a difficult term, these tools have the resources for greater depth and clarity. When you become familiar with these tools, you can use them effectively to enrich your study sessions and grow your knowledge of God's Word.

Tips for Selecting and Using These Bible Tools

Consider your preferences and study goals when deciding on Bible study tools and resources. Here are practical tips to help you choose and use these resources effectively to influence your Bible understanding significantly:

Start with a Solid Study Bible

Before considering other tools or resources, establish a proper foundation with a good study Bible. Unlike a standard Bible, a study Bible contains footnotes, maps, cross-references, and explanatory articles to understand verses or passages better. However, research the various translations and choose one that feels right and includes a comprehensive study aid that matches your knowledge and interest. As a beginner, choose one that's not theologically overwhelming but provides clear explanations. As you become more knowledgeable, you can switch to a study Bible that explores historical context or theological nuances.

Identify Your Study Goals

Knowing what you intend to achieve with these tools influences your choices. If you want to understand a verse or Bible principles daily, find a tool that does this. For example, if you aim to grasp the text's cultural background, a Bible commentary or historical background study guide would be more useful than a concordance. Also, if you want to explore how a word is used throughout the Bible, then a concordance or Bible dictionary would be your best pick. By clearly identifying and defining your study objectives, you can easily narrow your options and make an informed choice.

Gradually Expand Your Toolkit

You might become overwhelmed or caught in the web of the thousands of available resources. The only way to avoid this is to start with the basics, and over time, you can enlarge your toolkit when you have a better understanding of what you need. Always begin with a study Bible, then progress to a Bible dictionary. Later, you can include commentary. You can incorporate other online resources as you become accustomed to your study apps. Using this approach for your

Bible study journey will allow you to enjoy many tools without feeling pressured or overwhelmed. Study tools are encouraged, but if you are comfortable with only your study Bible, stick to it until you need more.

Consider Your Learning Style

Everyone has a learning style that works best for them, so it's a good idea to find out your learning style. People learn differently, and this will influence their choice of tools for their Bible study. For example, a visual learner will probably work best with charts, maps, and illustrated commentaries. An auditory learner should consider apps that offer audio versions of commentaries or sermons. Someone who loves writing should consider a Bible journal or a study guide with reflective questions. Choosing tools resonating with your preferred learning style enhances your comprehension, understanding, and retaining Bible knowledge.

Stay Flexible and Open-Minded

Do not be afraid to switch tools if something new suits your study objectives better. As you grow in your study of the Bible, you may notice your goals and interests change, and a tool you used regularly in the past may no longer be as useful. When you try different tools, you'll discover that you are opening yourself up to a more dynamic and enriching study experience.

The What-Is- and Value of Bible Tools

Not all Bible tools are helpful, so always vet their credibility and reliability to ensure accurate information. Various aspects to check when vetting these tools are things like the author's background, date and place of publication – and user reviews. Don't take their word for it – cross-check areas like their theological training, which denominations they are affiliated with, and their reputation within the Christian community. Scholarly resources from recognized institutions or well-respected theologians are more reliable. However, this doesn't rule out other great resources from unpopular authors. It's always safer to get recommendations.

Next, check the resource or tool's date of publication. While some older publications may give you valuable historical context, their information may not reflect modern research findings – balance older resources with more recent scholarly research. Look out for and avoid resources whose main objective is to push an agenda or has a clear bias in its explanation and interpretation. These might deviate from sound hermeneutical principles in their interpretations. So, use research tools that provide a balanced view and acknowledge the interpretations of a passage.

Lastly, always run a fact check by cross-referencing information with multiple sources. Consider it trustworthy if several known and credible sources agree on a particular fact or interpretation. You will build a solid foundation for your Bible study when you carefully evaluate each study tool.

When integrating multiple resources into your Bible study sessions, these several practical strategies can enhance your understanding and retention of scripture:

Create a Study Plan: Outline your goal for each study session. Then, decide which resource to use for specific passages or topics, a commentary for in-depth analysis or a Bible dictionary for word studies.

Layer Your Resources: Begin with a study Bible to help you get a general overview. Then, dive deeper using a commentary or concordance. Layering your study allows you to gradually build up your understanding.

Use a Study Journal: Consider a dedicated notebook to jot down points from each resource. It will help you track your learning when reviewing and reflecting.

Visual Aids and Charts: Get visual resources like timelines, maps, and charts from study Bibles or online tools to help you contextualize the Bible's historical events and make its complex information easier to grasp.

Scheduled Reflection Time: After using several resources, summarize what you've learned. Reflection enhances your understanding and reinforces new knowledge.

Cross-Resource Questions: Pose the same questions to various resources and compare the responses you get. For example, after you read a passage, consult a commentary to see how your Bible dictionary or another translation addressed the same verse. This method helps widen your understanding.

Group Study Sessions: Discuss all the results you received from the different resources with others in your study group. Sharing perspectives deepens your understanding and gives you new angles on familiar passages you previously missed.

You can learn so much from using Bible study tools and resources when studying God's Word. However, find one that suits you and will help you achieve your goal. Well done for making it this far. The future chapters promise more exciting knowledge, increasing your yearning to study God's Word. You can do this!

Chapter 6: Understanding Historical and Cultural Backgrounds in the Bible

You've covered much so far, from understanding the importance of a consistent Bible study routine to exploring the interpretation of several Bible translations. You've discovered tools and resources to make your study more effective and begun understanding how historical and cultural contexts impact your interpretation of Biblical texts. However, there's a deeper way to understand the scriptures in historical and cultural contexts. It's one thing to read the words on the page; it's another thing to understand what they meant to the people who first heard them. This understanding brings alive the Bible's richness and a more precise view.

Cultural and historical events will give more meaning to your study of the Bible.[18]

In this chapter, you'll learn more about the historical events, political climates, and cultural practices that influenced Biblical narratives. How you understand these aspects isn't only about acquiring more knowledge. It's about using them to connect deeply with scriptures by seeing them through the eyes for whom it was written. As you grow in your Bible study, this will help you interpret texts more accurately.

The Importance of Historical and Cultural Context

The only way to accurately interpret the Bible is through an understanding of its historical and cultural context. These contexts are essential for the following reasons:

It Clarifies the Original Meaning of Texts

The Bible was written at a particular time in history with a different culture from today. When a person doesn't understand the context surrounding these texts, it could lead to misinterpreting the message or failure to capture its intended message. For example, the "denarius" Jesus spoke about in the parable of the laborers in Matthew 20:1-16 was Roman laborers' daily wage. Knowing this clarifies the economic and social theme in this parable. Gaining more understanding of Biblical texts through the view of the original audience requires insight into their historical and cultural contexts. It enables the message to come alive and show its relevance to your life.

Prevents Misinterpretation

Misinterpretation is a common challenge when studying the Bible. For example, you might interpret some of Paul's teachings as harsh or outdated when you do not consider early Christian communities' social norms and issues. A clear understanding of their issues, like persecution, pagan practice influences, and others, will help you, as a 21st-century reader, to see the necessity of Paul's advice.

Illuminates the Significance of Events and Teachings

When you approach a passage from the historical and cultural context, it helps you see the significance of its teachings according to the events surrounding it. For example, the Exodus story about God's chosen people is not only about a physical journey. It's a powerful narrative of liberation and covenant, deeply rooted in ancient Israel's cultural and religious practices. Understanding their oppression under Pharaoh and the subsequent formation of a new identity as God's chosen people enriches the story.

Enhances Application to Modern Life

When you understand the Bible's teaching from its historical and cultural context, you easily grasp its significance in today's world. For example, knowing the role of women in first-century Judea can give you an informed understanding of how it applies to women in the church today. Instead of interpreting a passage at first glance, understand its historical backdrop for a more thoughtful application, respecting the original intent while addressing modern concerns.

Explains Symbolism and Metaphors

The Bible used symbolic language and metaphors in its messages to the original audience. Therefore, it could be slightly puzzling to a modern reader. For instance, when Jesus refers to Himself as the "Good Shepherd" (John 10:11), He uses the example of a traditional occupation in Israel where shepherds symbolize leadership and care. Similarly, phrases like "kingdom of heaven" or "mustard seed" make meaningful sense when viewed through the Jewish expectations of the Messiah and their agricultural practices. Understanding these symbols within their historical and cultural context reveals a deeper meaning.

Informs Doctrinal Understanding

Understanding historical background is essential for correct Bible teachings. For example, the Trinity isn't spelled out directly in the Bible., However, knowing how early Christians debated and taught about Jesus' divinity will help you understand this belief. By looking at the cultural context of when the New Testament was written, you can see how the belief in one God and Jesus' divine nature came together in Christian teaching.

Promotes Respect for the Text

Engaging with the Bible's historical and cultural context demonstrates a respect for Biblical texts and their origins. It allows you to acknowledge that the Bible was written by real people in real situations, addressing a specific audience with particular concerns. This acknowledgment can encourage you to be more careful and thoughtful in reading and interpreting scriptures and avoid the pitfalls of superficial or anachronistic readings.

A Discussion on Some of the Actual Cultural Contexts within the Old and New Testaments

Understanding the cultural contexts of the Old and New Testaments can enhance your comprehension of the Bible. Here are four examples, two from each testament, illustrating cultural background significance:

Covenant Rituals and Sacrifices

In the Old Testament, particularly in books like Leviticus, laws associated with sacrifices and covenant rituals reflected how the people of that time practiced their relationship with God. For instance, their animal sacrifices to atone for sins and achieve purity reflected culture, like those of the Canaanites and Egyptians. Understanding these practices helps you grasp why these rituals were significant and how they symbolized deeper spiritual truths about atonement and devotion.

The Role of Kingship

In the books of 1 and 2 Samuel, kingship in ancient Israel was influenced by surrounding nations in the Land of Canaan. The kings were seen as divinely appointed political figures who were expected to lead with justice and uphold religious laws. For example, the story of King David is framed by his role as a shepherd, reflecting Israel's idea of kingship and the cultural expectations of rulers.

New Testament Contexts

Roman Occupation and Governance

The events of the New Testament occurred during Roman rule in Judea. Understanding how political customs worked in those days will help you understand the New Testament text better. For example, the complexities of Roman laws and politics influenced the interactions between Jesus and Roman authorities like Pontius Pilate. The Roman Empire's influence on local governance and the social tension it created provides context for many New Testament narratives, including the reasons for Jesus' crucifixion and the early Christian community's struggles.

Hellenistic Influence

The New Testament was written when Greek culture, known as Hellenism, prevailed due to Alexander the Great's conquests. This influence is evident in the Greek language used in New Testament writings. For example, Paul's letters often engage with Greek philosophical ideas and rhetoric. He emphasized how he'd been called to preach. When you learn about the Hellenistic cultural environment, you'll know why themes, like the resurrection and Christ's nature, were addressed in ways that resonated with Greek-speaking audiences.

How Historical Events, Political Conditions, and Social Norms of Biblical Times Influence the Message and Interpretation of Scripture

Here is how these norms, events, and situations from Biblical times significantly impact your understanding of the Bible:

Historical Events: Major events like the Exodus and the Babylonian Exile shaped the Old Testament. During this period, the Israelites faced significant challenges, as reflected in books like Exodus, Numbers, and Lamentations. Learning about these events will help you see why themes like hope and restoration are highlighted in the Bible.

Political Conditions: Political events like Roman rule during the times of the New Testament affected the stories and teachings of the Bible. For example, the conflict that transpired between the Jewish and Roman leaders is evident in the Gospels. When you understand how these issues unfolded, you will know why themes like authority and justice are so central and popular in Jesus' teachings.

Social Norms: This greatly influences how you read the Bible. For example, the role of women in ancient society affects your knowledge of women's roles in the church today. Paul's letters often address these social issues; knowing what those issues were helps you interpret his messages correctly.

When you consider these historical, political, and social factors, you get a clearer picture of what the Bible meant to its original readers and how you can apply its teachings today.

Examples of Key Historical Periods and Events and How They Shape the Understanding of Specific Passages

Understanding key historical periods and events can significantly shape your understanding of Bible passages. A few notable examples are explored below:

Roman Occupation During the New Testament

During the times of events recorded in the New Testament, the Roman Empire controlled most parts of the world, including Judea. This rule influenced many aspects of daily life and the New Testament's message. For example, the Gospels often reflect the tension between the Jewish people and the Romans. Jesus' teachings about "rendering unto Caesar what belonged to Caesar" (Mark 12:17) and His interactions with Roman officials show the complex relationship between Jews and Romans. Knowing how the Romans ruled will help you understand why issues like taxation and political authority are central in New Testament passages. It sheds light on how early Christians, like

The Roman Empire and Caesar's effect on early Christian history is important to learn about.[14]

Paul, had to navigate their faith within a politically charged environment.

The Babylonian Exile

The Babylonian Exile was a pivotal event where many Israelites were captured and sent to Babylon after the fall of Jerusalem in 586 B.C. This event influenced the writing and themes of several Old Testament books, like Ezekiel, Daniel, 2 Kings, and Jeremiah. For example, the Book of Lamentations expresses Israel's deep sorrow over the destruction of Jerusalem and the loss of the temple. Recognizing this would help you better understand themes like mourning and hope for restoration. It explains why the prophets often spoke of God's promise to bring the Israelites back to their homeland – restoration.

The Egyptian Influence

Egypt played a major role in the Bible, especially in the story of Israel's slavery and their deliverance from bondage in Exodus. This story symbolizes the Jewish identity, focusing on themes like freedom, justice, and God's protection. The Exodus is central to the Jewish faith and still influences many practices, such as the celebration of Passover. Beyond the Exodus, Egyptian culture is reflected in other parts of the Bible, such as wisdom in Proverbs, which shares similarities with Egyptian teachings. Some Psalms and the portrayal of Pharaohs show traces of Egyptian influence.

Some Psalms and the portrayal of Pharaohs show the influence of ancient Egypt.[15]

Knowing Egypt's role in the Bible will help you understand the stories, Bible characters, and their meanings. For example, the plagues in Exodus weren't just signs and wonders. They were symbolic, challenging the power of Egyptian gods. Knowing this adds depth to your interpretation during Bible study. This background context helps you see how the Exodus story was later used to inspire hope during challenging times. For example, when the Israelites were exiled to Babylon.

The Persian Empire

The story of the Israelites, God's chosen people in the Book of Esther, gives insight into the culture and social dynamics of Jews living under foreign rule. It shows how the Jewish people managed their identity and faith in a population as a minority. They were often at risk of persecution and destruction from their neighbors. The political intrigue, the influence of royal decrees, and the role of women in the Persian court were crucial elements that shaped the narrative and its interpretation.

The story of Esther and the Israelites does not encourage a military revolt like the Maccabean Revolt. However, it reflects the theme of survival and deliverance during a period of foreign domination. The story underscores the importance of themes like faith, courage, belief in divine providence, and God's power in the face of external threats, which is central to the Jewish experience during exile and foreign rule.

Examining these historical periods and events gives you a deeper appreciation of the Bible's messages, helping you apply the scriptures more accurately to your life.

Cultural Practices, Beliefs, and Values and Their Impact on Biblical Interpretation

Cultural practices, beliefs, and values of the Bible help you interpret scriptures in today's world. A deep reading would reveal how frail human nature was and still is and how your faith is intertwined with the complexities of your culture, values, and beliefs. Knowing how they interacted with one another and with God gives a more profound insight into the Bible.

For instance, understanding concepts like honor and shame in ancient societies will change how you read scriptures. In Biblical times, honor was everything. It was about maintaining your family's reputation and standing in the community. This is why actions like David's defeat of Goliath were so significant. It wasn't just a victory over a giant. It restored Israel's honor in the face of humiliation by their enemies. Similarly, when Jesus spoke to or healed people who were outcasts, like the lepers or the woman caught in adultery, He wasn't only showing kindness. He challenged the social norms, confronting how society treated the dishonored.

David's defeat of Goliath.[16]

Another key example would be the practice of ritual purification, particularly in the Old Testament. For instance, many laws in Leviticus are about being ceremonially clean, essential for worship and community participation. Without understanding how important purity was to the Jewish people, it's easy to miss the significance of passages about Jesus touching the sick or the dead—acts that would have made Him ritually unclean by the standards of His time. Instead, Jesus' actions show a new way of relating with God, which portrayed compassion over ritual.

The covenant relationship between God and His people is another cultural element influencing your Biblical interpretation. In those times, covenants were serious agreements – sealed with rituals and sacrifices. The Bible uses this concept to describe God's relationship with Israel and later with the church. A good understanding explains why the scriptures talk so much about God's faithfulness and why breaking God's commandments is a severe betrayal. It sheds light on the New Testament's emphasis on the *new covenant through Jesus*, representing a new way for humanity to relate to God.

Learning about these and other cultural practices, beliefs, and values will help you read the Bible in a new and profound way and appreciate the depth and richness of its messages in their original context. It gives you a more precise direction to apply the teachings in your life today.

Practical Tips for Researching Historical and Cultural Backgrounds

Follow these tips for more accurate research:

Look for Archaeological Insights in Commentaries and Study Guides: Many Bible commentaries and study guides provide information from archaeology without you having to delve into complex studies. They support and illuminate stories of the Bible, and you benefit from archaeological knowledge without needing to be an expert.

Read Scholarly Journals and Articles: These are a rich source of information on Biblical history, archaeology, and cultural studies. These tools and resources give you the latest research and interpretations to enrich your understanding of the scriptures.

Participate in Bible Study Groups Focused on Historical Context: Joining a Bible study group emphasizing historical and cultural backgrounds will give you new perspectives and discussions, deepening your understanding.

Attend Lectures or Seminars: Look for opportunities to attend lectures, workshops, or seminars led by Biblical scholars or historians. These events will open your eyes to specific historical moments or cultural practices relevant to your study.

Use Online Courses and Video Lectures: Many online platforms offer courses and lectures on Biblical history and culture. It is a convenient way to learn structured knowledge at your own pace.

Explore Historical Novels or Documentaries: This would bring the cultural and historical background of the Bible to life more engagingly. They can encourage your hunger to seek more research.

Compare Bible Translations: Sometimes, reading various Bible translations helps reveal slight differences in language that reflect historical and cultural background. It can help you see how different translators have interpreted the same texts.

These strategies, combined with traditional study tools, will enhance your ability to research and understand the historical and cultural backgrounds of the Bible.

Suggestions for Incorporating Historical and Cultural Insight

Looking into texts and historical documents outside of the Bible can give you a richer and more fun experience with the scriptures. These tools and resources help you paint a picture of what life was like during Biblical times. When you look into them, you realize how their surroundings influenced the people and themes in the Bible. This additional background information makes the Bible's stories and teachings more relatable and easier to apply today.

Applying historical and cultural insights into your Bible study can enhance your understanding and application of scripture. Start by researching the background of the book or passage you're studying. Understand the historical events, cultural norms, and societal values when the text was written. Begin by reading the introduction sections in a good study Bible, which often provide historical and cultural context. Then, pair this with commentaries that go into the customs, politics, and religious practices. When you come across a particular cultural practice or event, look it up in a Bible dictionary or online research. This research can clarify why certain actions or words were significant.

Another suggestion is to reflect on how these cultural practices differ from or relate to today. You will see the timeless principles in scripture and apply them more effectively in your life. For instance, understanding hospitality in ancient times can deepen your grasp of passages that talk about welcoming others.

Lastly, write down your findings. Consider how historical and cultural context changes your understanding of a passage and how it might influence your actions or beliefs. When you incorporate this into your study routine regularly, you'll appreciate the Bible's message better.

There's much beauty and fascination when you truly delve into what life was like during Biblical times. It gives you a balanced understanding and helps you to know what these characters felt in their positions and situations. It is a good way to build faith in God because the characters are no longer fictional or like otherworldly beings. You can tell they are human, walked on this Earth, and trusted God.

Chapter 7: Recognizing Themes in the Bible

In the Bible, God revealed Himself to people differently. Biblical themes center around God's personality and how He planned His ways from creation. Through the scriptures, you find that God loved, provided, protected, judged, delivered, gave His promises, and created covenants with men, which explains His nature. The Bible tells of the events that happened to men in the light of God's nature. Interestingly, even in this modernized world, the Word of God has not lost its essence or power. God revealed those attributes of Himself to counter the nature and character of mankind. God chose those attributes (referred to in this chapter as themes) to reconcile Himself to mankind, redeem them, give them a new heart and life – and, most importantly, create a new covenant through the blood of Christ. The Bible is built upon numerous themes. This chapter explores a few and teaches you how to recognize more.

When you read the Bible, you will find relatable themes.[17]

The Concept of Themes in the Bible

The Bible is a tapestry of timeless teachings and wisdom told through stories and characters. It has shaped culture, inspired extraordinary acts, guided moral principles, and inspired many supernatural experiences for millions all over the world. Within its pages, the foundation of human existence is found. For example, the existence of the most populous race on earth was birthed by one man's obedience, Abraham. God's covenant with him gave him the fulfillment of a promise that is still in play today.

The scripture says in Genesis 17:

"... you will be called Abraham, for you will be the father of many nations. I will make you extremely fruitful. Your descendants will become many nations, and kings will be among them! "I will confirm my covenant with you and your descendants after you, from generation to generation. This is the everlasting covenant: I will always be your God and the God of your descendants after you." - Genesis 17:5-7 NLT

The word "covenant" isn't an experience shared by Abraham alone. Other men of faith encountered God via covenants. Therefore, the Word reveals a side of God relating to men and explains the concept of a theme. In the Bible, themes are reoccurring ideas and messages often interwoven through scriptures, making them connect various stories, passages, and books. They help you understand how God relates with humanity. It's in the themes' context that godly principles and religious beliefs were birthed. This is evident in the verse that follows God's covenant with Abraham:

"Then God said to Abraham, "Your responsibility is to obey the terms of the covenant. You and all your descendants have this continual responsibility... Each male among you must be circumcised." – Genesis 17:9-10 NLT

These themes help you understand how God often relates to humanity, and they reveal how you should relate with others based on your Christian faith. These Biblical themes teach that God is Sovereign and forever in control of times and seasons, wielding them for His good will and purpose.

Major Biblical Themes and How They Occur in Scriptures

The Bible isn't a mere collection of people's art or random stories. Even though it may feel this way sometimes. It might be hard to relate to the characters or why God demands a certain lifestyle. Amid this confusion, you will observe patterns and common themes. Major themes like love, redemption, justice, faith, and covenant reoccur throughout the Old and New Testament. These themes offer insight into man's imperfections and God's unconditional and consistent intervention.

Here are five biblical themes and how they occur in the scriptures:

Love

The scripture portrays love as the essence of God's character. It defines His selflessness toward mankind in a life-giving relationship. You will discover numerous values or levels of the word "love" in the Old Testament. For example, the Hebrew word *khesed*, translated as "loyal love," and *ahavah* as an "affectionate or caring love," shows the different expressions of one word. Further into the Bible, you learn about the Greek term for love, "*agape*," meaning "divine love," and *philia*, "familial love," which are different ways God and people of old expressed love. God expressed His love for His people through faithfulness, mercy, compassion, grace, and His commandments.

See what the scripture says in Psalms 89:

"If they do not obey my decrees and fail to keep my commands, then I will punish their sin with the rod... But I will

never stop loving him nor fail to keep my promise to him. No, I will not break my covenant; I will not take back a single word I said." Psalms 89:31-34 NLT

God's nature never changes, and this theme continued after Jesus' birth and death. It was the foundation of Jesus' sacrifice for mankind.

"But God commendeth his love toward us, in that, while we were yet sinners, Christ died for us." – Romans 5:8 KJV

Studying to discover the love of God is relatively easy within this context. The scriptures help you shine more light on this theme. To understand God's love expressed through different characters and men of faith, study these scriptures while applying the understanding you now have:

- God's love towards Israel (Deuteronomy 7:7-8, Isaiah 43:4)
- The story of Hosea and Gomer (Hosea 1-3)
- Jesus' teachings on love (Matthew 22:37-40, John 13:34-35)
- The sacrifice of Jesus as a demonstration of God's love (John 3:16, Romans 5:8)

Redemption

This is an exceptional and divinely orchestrated theme in the Bible. It spans the New and Old Testaments. It explains the wisdom and intelligence of God portrayed from the time of the creation of the world. Redemption is an act that explains recovery, payment to buy back, and sacrifice to free one from bondage, which was the reason behind the birth of the church. When Adam and Eve sinned in the Garden of Eden, God had already planned to recover the relationship He once shared with man. This can be seen through the various instructions and commandments given to the Israelites, from the Exodus to the fulfillment of those commandments and prophecies in the New Testament and on through the death of Jesus. Look at a vivid example of God redeeming His people through the covenant He made with Abraham and maintained until Jacob's generation, Abraham's grandson. God reveals through this text that one man's righteousness can atone for the lives of the unborn, which He demonstrated with the Israelites. It was the righteous act of their ancestor that made them worthy to be called God's people.

Look at what scripture says about Abraham:

"For the scriptures tell us, "Abraham believed God, and God counted him as righteous because of his faith." Romans 4:3 NLT

So, you could say that redemption came to a group of people because of one man's faith. Does this phrase sound familiar? Yes, the apostle Paul wrote about the sacrifice of Christ when he said:

" Yes, Adam's one sin brings condemnation for everyone, but Christ's one act of righteousness brings a right relationship with God and new life for everyone." Romans 5:18 NLT

Redemption is God's intervention to deliver His people from sin and its consequences. To trace redemption more, study these scriptures:

- The Exodus from Egypt (Exodus 1-15)
- The story of Ruth and Naomi (Ruth 1-4)
- Jesus' teachings on redemption (Luke 4:18-19, Galatians 3:13-14)
- The sacrifice of Jesus as a means of redemption for man (Ephesians 1:7, Hebrews 9:12)

Justice

Humans are made in the image and likeness of God, and by nature, mankind is given dominance over every other creature. Hence, humans must judge other creatures based on God's Justice.

Humans must only judge others using God's justice.[18]

It says in Genesis 1:26:

"Then God said, "Let us make human beings in our image, to be like us...."

"To be like us" doesn't describe facial, characteristics, and personality only. It signifies authority and power to exhibit God's attributes. The Bible describes justice as a term in Hebrew, "*mishpat*" meaning "restorative justice," which frequently appeared in the Old Testament. God's definition of justice is helping the oppressed and standing up for those who cannot speak for themselves. These reform the social construct to stop other injustices.

It says in the scriptures:

"Learn to do good. Seek justice. Help the oppressed. Defend the cause of orphans. Fight for the rights of widows." - Isaiah 1:17 NLT.

He commands through the prophet Micah:

"He hath shewed thee, O man, what is good; and what doth the LORD require of thee, but to do justly, and to love mercy, and to walk humbly with thy God?" - Micah 6:8 KJV

To understand the concept of justice more, study these scriptures:

- The Law and its emphasis on justice (Exodus 20-23, Leviticus 19)

- Jesus' teachings on justice (Matthew 25:31-46, Luke 4:18-19)

- The importance of justice in the early Christian community (Acts 6:1-7, James 1:27)

Faith

Many believe faith is a belief or complete trust in God. Is that only what it is? As you've read under redemption, one man's faith stood as a testament centuries after his death. To fully understand faith, you must observe the lives of forerunners of faith. Hebrews 11 has a list of individuals with a common theme or attribute among them – obedience. Amid misunderstanding and confusion, obedience requires your absolute devotion and immediate response to His will. This is the living sacrifice Paul talked about in Romans 12:1. Remember, belief without obedience is not faith (James 1:22), and sacrifice after disobedience is not faith. Faith is the only attribute that moves God's heart.

"And it is impossible to please God without faith..." Hebrews 11:6 NLT

You can search the following passages to understand faith better to recognize it in other passages:

- The story of Abraham and Sarah (Genesis 12-21)
- The story of Moses and the Exodus (Exodus 1-15)
- Jesus' teachings on faith (Matthew 17:20, Mark 11:22-24)
- The importance of faith in the early Christian community (Hebrews 11, James 2:14-26)

Covenant

Covenant allows a person to relate with God on a sacrificial scale. For example, it entails agreeing with God to give up a part of yourself to be used wholly by God. In return, He unfolds a nature of Himself to you. God created and established many covenants to sustain the world He created. Some men of faith who willingly went into a covenant with God are Noah, Abraham, Jacob, Aaron, David, and Jephthah. Examples of those born into a covenant or dedicated from birth include Samson, Samuel, Moses, John the Baptist, and Jesus (The New Covenant).

The following scriptures will help you understand what forms the theme 'Covenant.'

- The Abrahamic Covenant (Genesis 12-21)
- The Mosaic Covenant (Exodus 19-24)
- The New Covenant in Jesus' blood (Luke 22:20, Hebrews 8:6-13)
- The importance of covenant faithfulness (Romans 9-11, Galatians 3-4)

These themes occur throughout the Bible, demonstrating God's consistent character and nature over periods and contexts.

Why Themes are Important and How They Can Be Applied Daily

The Bible isn't only what you read to learn about the life of God. It's the manuscript you study to learn about your new life in God. Several themes have been explored in this chapter. However, you must first understand why they exist to apply them daily. Themes give direction and purpose to your study, meaning to ideas and passages, offer a new perspective in reading scriptures, and inspire and motivate you by revealing your possibilities as God's child.

How can you apply them daily? Take them one at a time. Start by reflecting on one theme – study the related scriptures, identify areas of your life where they can apply (relationship, career, mindset), discuss them with others for insight, and live by them.

Practical Methods for Identifying Themes within Passages

Follow the methods below to practicalize theme identification in the Bible:

Find a Topic

You can use a regular Bible, but study Bibles are specifically for studying because they provide basic tools for easier studying. After the book of Revelations in a study Bible is a new section called "Index" or "Parenthesis." This section is a great start if you've not decided on a theme to study. Themes in the index are arranged alphabetically and cover most familiar issues. Under each issue are scriptural texts where they apply to Bible characters and stories. This is one way to find a theme.

A second way is during your study hours. For example, when reading Romans and you come across the theme of contentment, search for other words relating to it before learning more about it, allowing for more texts. The third way is observing and journaling the themes that stand out in a chapter during your study hours. It provides you with more ideas for those times.

Search Related Words and Synonyms

After identifying your theme, look up synonyms and related words. You may use antonyms when the theme's context is negative. For example, for "'fear," you could study themes like peace, love, and joy.

Use The Right Tools

Now that you have a list of words in your journal, research scriptures covering each word. There are several tools to enhance your research, like the exhaustive concordance, which makes finding words and every related text associated with them easier. Another helpful tool is a topical Bible, which, like a study Bible, arranges Bible themes and topics alphabetically – for example, the Thompson Chain Reference Bible. A cross-reference Bible is helpful in identifying and expanding themes.

Observe Each Passage

Read each passage to see what it says about your given theme. Are there patterns of instructions, commands, promises, or warnings following it? Who are the text's authors, and what circumstances surround the author and audience? These help ensure you read the verses within context.

Put Your Findings Together

Combine your notes, marked scriptures, and written instructions. You can sub-categorize your theme for better comprehension and further study. For instance, place negative verses together and counter them with positive verses. Summarize your observations for better ways to apply them in your life.

Here are other questions to help you organize your summary:

- How does this theme apply today?
- How does it affect me, and what area of my life does it address?
- How does it affect the church?
- How would this change things around me?
- How did my view of a situation change after I studied this theme?
- Does this theme help me understand God better?
- Would this theme improve how I relate with people in my immediate environment?
- Could I measure my growth over time?

For better results, trace your theme across other books of the Bible to see the author's views and how often they appeared in those books. For example, the crucifixion of Jesus was written in more detail by Apostle John, as he was the only disciple who followed Jesus from His arrest until His crucifixion. Mathew significantly recorded Jesus' works. The various Bible study tools will help you learn these contexts better. However, in your quest to apply each theme, you need a system for accountability. It could be with a friend, family, religious mentor, or a study group. Accountability creates room for assessment, which helps you track yourself.

Chapter 8: Applying Scripture to Everyday Life

The best way to preserve knowledge is by applying it. For example, how does someone say they have read a book? Is it only by saying it? Of course not. It's by living according to the book's principles. Many have read the Bible from cover to cover but don't experience the expected transformation because they fail to apply the principles. It's in application that you experience the essence of God's Word. This chapter provides practical steps to apply scriptures daily and tips to overcome major Bible application setbacks.

The goal is to be able to apply what you learn in everyday life.[19]

The Importance of Applying Scriptures in Everyday Life

You can consider the Bible as a relevant text and believe its principles for a great life, but its relevance only doesn't necessarily teach you how to apply it to daily living. Similarly, reading stories from the Bible gives you an idea of its character's experience and illustrates how someone from long ago managed something like what you may be experiencing. You may feel empathy toward that character because you share the same experience. However, this doesn't guarantee you will get the same breakthrough result as the character. Remember, the Bible is not a storybook. All scriptures are inspired by God. There is a central theme that stands no matter the scripture you read: "Living a Christ-centered life is the purpose for human existence, and in return, God is the reward for this lifestyle."

God rewards every effort you put into growing your faith. However, efforts alone won't stand the test of time. Instead, relying on God's strength to uphold you as you carry on this quest is key to standing the test of time. God says in His Word:

"He gives power to the weak and strength to the powerless." -
Isaiah 40:29 NLT

Application begins with study, but it doesn't end there, even when studying feels tedious, tasking, and boring. Application is where you exercise your study muscles. It gives you room to *do* the *what* part, to focus on the truth of God's Word, and to respond to your understanding of scripture. Application is a choice and makes it personal. Through it, you gain knowledge.

The scriptures describe what happens when you strive to understand scriptures:

"...Pay close attention to what you hear. The closer you listen,
the more understanding you will be given—and you will receive
even more." - Mark 4:24 NLT

It explains the importance of honing scriptural application skills:

"Solid food is for those who are mature, who through training
have the skill to recognize the difference between right and
wrong." - Hebrews 5:14 NLT

Solid food means the word of God, which, when consumed, gives you spiritual stamina. It gives you maturity in the spirit, and like God, you can discern right from wrong. Mankind has many flaws in its imperfect nature, but the Bible remains your guide to living an abundant life. Daily living by God's Word is required in your Christian race. It is what drives you to rely wholly on God.

Biblical Principles and How They Influence Your Life

You can study the scriptures in an inductive or deductive way. In an inductive study of the word, you read without a preconceived idea of the context, opening your mind to allow the word of God to speak to you freely. In these Biblical principles, your mind is open and not easily drawn to a conclusion as you gather your clues to piece them all together. You study to learn and understand, not to prove a point. For example, when reading about the life of David, specifically the event between David and Goliath in 1 Samuel 17, ask these questions:

- What does this passage say about David's attitude toward Goliath?

- What role did God play?

- Can I emulate David's actions in my life? In which area can I achieve that?

Notice how these questions give you an open view of the scripture, giving you room to learn from David's lifestyle and character. However, a deductive study of the Bible is quite different. u already have an idea, and you only need scriptures to back it up. You search the Bible for verses to support your idea and brood over them for a better understanding. Unlike the inductive, which makes you think like a detective, the deductive makes you think like a lawyer, looking for evidence to prove your case.

A practical example would be how you believe God wants people to be rich and live abundantly. So, you search the Bible for verses supporting this idea, like Psalm 112:3: "*They themselves will be wealthy, and their good deeds will last forever.*" Reading the scripture this way might lead you to ignore other verses suggesting wealth and riches aren't the most important things (Matthew 19:24, 1 Timothy 6:10).

You see here how your thinking pattern can influence your daily life, self-worth, relationship, and growth, positively or otherwise. Adjusting your mindset to accommodate God's Word will positively influence every aspect of your life. The more room you give, the more God's Word overshadows your mindset, and eventually, you're transformed into a new individual. This change doesn't end with you because the people around you will notice and get affected. So, besides a personal transformation from applying God's Word, you also enjoy better relationships.

Micah 6:8 explains how to live:

> *"He has shown you, O man, what is good; And what does the Lord require of you but to do justly, to love mercy and to walk humbly with your God?" (NKJV)*

This affects your decision-making. What influences your decisions? Were they influenced by God's Word? Analyzing your decisions this way leads to applying the word, making a difference in your spiritual journey.

Here's another scripture that aids your decision-making process:

> *"Jesus replied, "'You must love the Lord your God with all your heart, all your soul, and all your mind.' This is the first and greatest commandment." - Matthew 22:37-38 NLT*

What do you think the world would look like if everyone applied this scripture? It doesn't have to be everyone. It could begin with you. Applying this scripture daily will change your world significantly. You'll carefully ensure that every decision is the mind of God to you, which will affect your life positively.

Practical Steps for Applying Scriptures

Here are four practical steps you can apply to make the scriptures a part of your daily life:

Observation Stage

> *"My son, give me thine heart, and let thine eyes observe my ways." - Proverbs 23:26 KJV*

Observation involves watching closely while paying attention to details with the aim of arriving at a judgment. Imagine you're reading a passage for the first time and find it hard to grasp the text's context. You need to read it a few times to understand the central idea. A few questions will help you in the observation stage, so ensure you have a journal to write your question and create a column for the answers: Who are the characters involved in this passage? What are their roles? What leads to these events? When did this occur? What happened afterward? Was this the fulfillment of a prophecy? When was this foretold, and by whom? The observation stage is where you patiently get a good understanding of the passage. In this stage, you do not read speedily, give up easily, make a judgment, or modify a verse to suit your reasoning.

Here's a scripture from 1 Corinthians 13:1-7 to make this more practical:

> *"If I could speak all the languages of earth and of angels, but didn't love others, I would only be a noisy gong or a clanging cymbal. If I had the gift of prophecy, and if I understood all of God's secret plans and possessed all knowledge, and if I had such faith that I could move mountains, but didn't love others, I would be nothing. If I gave everything I have to the poor and even sacrificed my body, I could boast about it, but if I didn't love others, I would have gained nothing."*

To answer the questions on the observation stage, you'll learn that this is Paul's first letter to the church in Corinth. He gives them a definition of love from his observation of them over time. He begins by telling them what love is **not** and that gifts and sacrifice are not evidence that someone has love. Then, he tells them what love is.

> *"...Love is patient and kind. Love is not jealous or boastful or proud or rude. It does not demand its own way. It is not irritable, and it keeps no record of being wronged. It does not rejoice about injustice but rejoices whenever the truth wins out. Love never gives up, never loses faith, is always hopeful, and endures through every circumstance."*

Love is patient and kind. What does it mean to be patient and kind? The next stage has the answer.

Interpretation Stage

In this stage, you read the scripture to search for clues to help you find answers to your questions.

Going back to verse 4 of 1 Corinthians 10, *"Love is patient and kind. Love is not jealous or boastful or proud or rude."* What did Paul intend to tell us about these virtues? It may mean that love is not only a feeling. It's an action, a way of living. There is no patience and kindness outside love, and there is no love outside patience and kindness. Does it also mean that when you exhibit characteristics like pride, rudeness, jealousy, and ego, they don't have love in them? Notice how plain and direct this verse was initially. When you interpret the scripture, you'll be exposed to its hidden truths and deeper meaning. In the observation stage, you're taught not to modify the context of the Bible to fit into your usual way of reasoning (like a deductive study). Instead, you must adjust your beliefs to align with God's Word.

To further interpret this verse, follow this order:

Research the meaning of the words that stood out to you. Determine which definition best fits the context in the verse.

- Consider the grammar. What two words were put together and why? Would they have meant something entirely different if used differently?

- Why did the author, Paul, write this way for that church?

- Use your Bible tools - dictionary, concordance, maps, encyclopedia

- How would you react to this text if it were communicated directly to you?

Meditation Stage

"Study this Book of Instruction continually. Meditate on it day and night so you will be sure to obey everything written in it. Only then will you prosper and succeed in all you do." - Joshua 1:8 NLT

Meditation is an essential part of your Bible study journey. It's in meditation that hidden things about scriptures are revealed by God. It requires focusing your mind on God's Word. Here's how God instructs meditating on His Word:

"And you must commit yourselves wholeheartedly to these commands that I am giving you today. Repeat them again and again to your children. Talk about them when you are at home and when you are on the road, when you are going to bed and when you are getting up. Tie them to your hands and wear them on your forehead as reminders. Write them on the doorposts of your house and on your gates." - Deuteronomy 6:6-9 NLT

Meditation requires focus to find the answers to your questions.[20]

Meditation requires asking and answering questions yourself. Examples of questions you can brood upon when meditating on a verse on love are:

- How can I show patience and kindness in my relationship?

- Are there areas in my life where I need to let go of pride and envy?

- What does this teach me about God's love for me?

- Is there anyone I've hurt through my arrogance and ignorance?

Application Stage

The application is where you exercise your Bible study muscles, without it, Bible study will be nothing more than an intellectual exercise. Ensure you only apply scriptures when you understand their meaning in context through observation, interpretation, meditation, and prayer. Prayer gives God room to supply you with the strength and wisdom to put His Word to work.

Here are steps as you learn to apply 1 Corinthians 10:4:

- Practice patience and kindness in a difficult relationship.

- Ask God to help you let go of pride and envy, jealousy, and rudeness.

- Remember God's kind love toward you and give thanks to Him.

Think about these scriptures and scenarios where you can apply them:

"Be kind to one another, tender-hearted, forgiving each other, just as God in Christ also has forgiven you." - Ephesians 4:32

"Forgive us our debts, as we also have forgiven our debtors." - Matthew 6:12

"Do not be conformed to the pattern of this world, but be transformed by the renewing of your mind. Then you will be able to test and approve what God's will is—his good, pleasing and perfect will." - Romans 12:2

Challenges in Applying Scriptures and How to Overcome Them

You may encounter a few challenges when applying scriptures, like misunderstanding or misinterpretation. The reasons for these challenges are:

- Handling scriptures incorrectly. Sometimes, you may use a text out of its original context. This can be fixed with the correct understanding of the text.

- Vague passages written to a different audience. You may find scriptures difficult to understand early in your study. It may be because the text was written to suit a specific audience. Hence, understanding the cultural context is vital.

- Doctrines and preconceptions. Sometimes, an ideology or revelation from God's Word may cause you to ignore other scriptures' realities. This is dangerous as it clouds your judgment and interpretation of God's Word.

- Difficult passages. You may have the urge to avoid some books of the Bible because of difficulty comprehending them. For example, the chronological order of Israel and Judah's kings.

To overcome these, you must study the Bible in language origin, literary, historical, and cultural context. Also, before interpretation, compare passages with other scriptures for differences and similarities. More importantly, use your Bible study tools.

Five Ways to Deepen Your Spiritual Journey

- **Seek Guidance from Spiritual Mentors:** A pastor or a trusted spiritual friend can offer you counsel, wisdom, and support for this quest.

- **Pray:** Developing a consistent prayer life cannot be over-emphasized. It helps you connect with God, share your worries and your thoughts with Him, and listen for guidance. Prayer gives you comfort and provides clarity and strength.

- **Join a Faith Community:** It could be a small group, a church, or an online community of believers. Grow with them and share your thoughts for guidance.

- **Reflect on Scriptures Often:** Read and study the Bible regularly and apply the principle of meditation.

- **Practice Journaling:** Write down your experiences – every challenge you faced, how you overcame them, and the methods and principles you applied. Journaling will be highly beneficial in the future.

Highlight on the Long-Term Benefit of Integrating Biblical Teaching

It has been frequently mentioned in this book that Biblical teachings far exceed simply enjoying the stories, cultures, and histories of the Bible characters. The reason they were put together, and you're encouraged to read them, is to understand the heart behind each story, letter, and scene to imbibe the lessons into your life. The Bible wasn't given to increase your knowledge but to change your life. This change is all-encompassing and real; it's not a moment caused by an adrenaline rush but a detailed step-by-step change that touches every area of your life. It's okay to call this change a long-term benefit because it never ends. Consider these benefits:

Personal Growth

The Bible in Romans 12: 2 and Proverbs 16:3 says:

"And do not be conformed to this world, but be transformed by the renewing of your mind, that you may prove what is that good and acceptable and perfect will of God." (NKJV)

And,

"Commit to the Lord whatever you do, and he will establish your plans" (NIV)

It's everyone's desire to become better as they age. The only way to achieve this is by constantly reviewing your actions, character, decisions, and attitude to fit a higher standard you've seen and set for yourself. This achievement can only happen through constant learning and practice. The Bible comprises many scriptures that guide transformation. When you spend time with scripture and apply it in your life, it will constantly change your mindset. Undoubtedly, a physical manifestation of your inner transformation will occur. A popular saying agrees that change begins from the mind. The Bible teaches that relying on God will help you actualize your plans. So, when you set a standard, the scriptures fill you with faith in God to meet it.

Improved Relationship

When you're interested in integrating Biblical teachings into your life, you'll find your relationships will be affected because a core theme of the Bible is love – love for yourself and others. When you imbibe a love habit and treat others equally, you will enjoy beautiful relationships with family, friends, neighbors, strangers, colleagues, or even unfriendly people. Besides love, every other theme in the Bible leads toward a better relationship between mankind and God – and between man and mankind. Look at some Bible verses that, when integrated, will transform your relationships:

John 17:3 (NKJV); *"And this is eternal life, that they may know you, the only true God, and Jesus Christ whom you have sent."*

Mark 12:31 (NKJV); "You *shall Love your neighbor as yourself."*

Proverbs 15:1 (NKJV); *"A soft answer turns away wrath, but a harsh word stirs up anger."*

Matthew 6:14-15 (NKJV); *"For if you forgive others their trespasses, your heavenly Father will also forgive you, but if you do not forgive others their trespasses, neither will your Father forgive your trespasses."*

There is so much to learn from the Bible to improve your relationships. The more time you spend, the more wisdom you gain for relationships, and the more examples you can use as a benchmark for your life.

A More Fulfilling Life

The goal for everyone is to live a fulfilling life, but people have different ideas of what fulfillment means. What is a fulfilled life for a Christian differs from a non-Christian's point of view. However, one thing is certain: the only true fulfillment in life is not based on material or personal possessions but on the eternal value of your relationship with God. The only way to attain this is by knowing God's will for your relationship with Him and everyone you encounter and your role in that will. Only in Bible study can you know this will. Consider Ephesians 5:17 (NIV); *"Therefore do not be foolish, but understand what the Lord's will is."* This scripture clarifies that anything besides understanding the will of God is foolishness. There's no way you can consider foolishness as fulfilling.

Integrating these Bible teachings is the only way to build yourself up to fit your role in His will. Consider the verse in Acts 20: 32 (ESV): *"And now I commend you to God and to the word of his grace, which is able to build you up and to give you the inheritance among all those who are sanctified."*

You'll agree that these benefits cannot be short-lived. They cover every aspect of life, and you'll enjoy them so long as you stay on the path they cover.

Scriptures give you godly inspiration, wisdom, counsel, and instructions for your life. They come in many ways, studying the word, teachings, counsel from mentors, songs, and even hymns. When you have an open mind toward your growth, applying scriptures is easy.

Chapter 9: Building a Bible Study Community

Spiritual growth is personal. It's a decision to begin, stay on course, and complete the journey. It doesn't exclude others on this journey. God made man a social being from the beginning when He created Adam. Even God socializes. He is a social being. The Trinity throughout the Bible, especially in the New Testament, describes the relationship between God the Father, the Son, and the Holy Spirit. God cherished the relationship so much that He didn't end it there but extended it to mankind. He demonstrated this in the story of salvation when He sent Jesus to Earth to relate with mankind. In the after-salvation story, He sent His Spirit to live inside those who extend their hand to Him for closer communion, revealing one of God's major goals: creating a community of Christians. As you grow and learn to cherish God's Word in your heart, you will realize you have questions that need answers and worries that need to be understood by someone who shares your goals. Community is where it begins.

Finding a community helps you share ideas.³¹

In a Bible study community, a group of people get together to encourage each other, discuss God's Word, pray together, counsel each other, and hold one another accountable in faith. The church was founded in the New Testament on community. It was relevant then, and it remains relevant today. This chapter teaches you about the benefits of studying the Bible in a community, how to find one near you, and gives practical ways to set up one yourself – along with tips to make it fun and engaging.

Benefits of Studying the Bible in a Community

"Let us think of ways to motivate one another to acts of love and good works. And let us not neglect our meeting together, as some people do, but encourage one another, especially now that the day of his return is drawing near." – Hebrews 10:24-25 NLT

Bible study enlightens and gives you wisdom toward life, but above all, it sparks questions about applying God's Word. When you are part of a community that lives by faith, understands spiritual principles, or perhaps is at the beginning of its journey, like you, you feel safe. A Bible community is for fellowship. Here are the benefits of studying the Bible with a community of Christians.

Diverse Perspectives

You could peek into someone's life experience through their words, thought patterns, and actions. These are influenced by past experiences, which have formed coping mechanisms to adjust to life. This is why people have opinions and interpret things differently. It is not something to worry about when joining a Christian community because, no matter the personal differences, every member has one goal: to learn and live the life of Jesus. When you have questions about a Bible text, someone will have had the same experience, gained wisdom from the text, learned lessons, and lived that scripture. Often, people in a community are open and excited to share their perspectives. However, you might not always agree with their view, but listening with an open heart can lead you closer to your answers or show you a better way to research answers.

When you exercise patience, you can learn from anyone. Here's a real-life example: a lady shares how she's been deeply impacted by a Christian community. She saw the gospel in a new light through her fellow Christian community members as they shared experiences with work-related issues. She faced challenges in the community, like disagreeing with others on mundane matters, even when they all share core values, but she understood that life is not perfect, and she needed to practice forgiveness to experience the power of grace.

Here's what the scripture says about accommodating others in Colossians 3:12-15 NLT:

> ".... you must clothe yourselves with tender-hearted mercy, kindness, humility, gentleness, and patience. Make allowance for each other's faults, and forgive anyone ...the Lord forgave you, so you must forgive others. Above all, clothe yourselves with love, which binds us all together in perfect harmony. And let the peace that comes from Christ rule in your hearts. For as members of one body, you are called to live in peace. And always be thankful."

Mutual Encouragement

A Bible study community allows you to be around people with different levels of faith. Knowing this assures you that you're not alone. It's through community that men like Barnabas became partners and friends with Paul. Timothy became Paul's spiritual son, and Silas was a companion in Paul's quest to spread the gospel to the gentile nations. A community is the first place you show behavioral change because as you associate with people who understand and apply Biblical truths, you get encouraged in your spiritual journey.

The scripture talks about this association in Proverbs 27:17 NKJV:

"As iron sharpens iron, So, a man sharpens the countenance of his friend."

Association matures your faith because you see lives transformed by taking in God's principles. You see and hear firsthand from people who faced a challenge you're going through and how they overcame it. A Bible study community is your new home or safe haven.

Here's a story of a lady who found support and encouragement from her Christian community: Judith, her husband, and their 1-year-old son relocated to a new country. Her husband practiced surgical procedures as an intern, and she obtained her PhD in neuroscience. They joined a Christian community but felt uncomfortable initially because it was outside their comfort zone. They often retreated home early because they preferred their privacy. Over time, they surrendered to the supportive and encouraging atmosphere, growing to love the community members. Although she had difficulty attending due to her husband's residency schedule, it didn't stop the members from visiting her whenever they could.

Accountability

When you get valuable instruction and insight from your Bible study, the next step is application. You are required to create measurable goals. Making this goal realistic might be challenging as a beginner, but you could seek proper guidance from experienced members if you're in a community. A benefit of group study is that it creates a platform where members hold each other accountable to work out principles learned individually or taught in a group. In this environment, you'll have open discussions and support for your challenges, struggles, misunderstandings, and other areas.

Jesus sets this example. See Luke 2:42,46:

"And when He was twelve years old, they went up to Jerusalem according to the custom of the feast..."

"...Now so it was that after three days they found Him in the temple, sitting in the midst of the teachers, both listening to them and asking them questions."

From a young age, Jesus sought a community of people with depths of knowledge of the scriptures. He sat amid teachers, listening and asking questions. If you read the scriptures further, you will see the consistency of His character. He created a community of believers as He called disciples to follow Him (Matthew 4:18-22); He visited His friends Martha and Mary, siblings of Lazarus, shared meals with them, and taught in their home (Luke 10:38-42). When He left Earth, this community continued with His disciples and others (Acts 1:13-14). Jesus says where two or three are gathered in His name, He is there (Matthew 18:20).

Finding Existing Bible Study Groups Around You

Finding a Bible study group is an enriching and fulfilling experience. The available options are online and offline. Below are steps to guide you:

What Are Your Bible Study Goals and Preferences?

What are your preferences as a part of a group? Are you okay with larger crowds, or do you prefer smaller gatherings? Are you comfortable in an unfamiliar environment, or do you need a community you're familiar with? What spiritual goals do you have? Are you only interested in being with Christians, with a community that would help deepen your theological knowledge, or with one that supports your journey? Considering your preferences, would an online meeting be better than an in-person meeting? Consider these as you work toward finding a Bible study community. Your goals will drive you to create a schedule to help attain your spiritual results.

Research Religious Groups or Local Churches

If you don't have any idea where to find physical Bible study groups, search for local churches and religious groups. Many churches have Bible study groups during the week or Sunday evenings. Visit the church's website to research meeting times, days, locations, and group leaders. See if it matches your schedule. Another way of becoming a part of a community is by attending services. So, join a church that teaches God's Word in depth, and after a service, you can approach the pastor or a leader to inquire about Bible study groups. Pay attention during the announcements because these details are usually mentioned via bulletins, newsletters, or during service.

Use Online Platforms

These days, anything can be found online. Multiple Bible study groups are available on numerous platforms as they often use this means to advertise or promote upcoming events and activities. If a physical meeting doesn't suit your schedule, try virtual. You can find them on platforms like Facebook, telegram, or Instagram. You could also search directly through your browser. They have websites where you can register as a member of their online group. Besides online websites, you can also access Bible study groups via sites like ChurchFinder.com and Biblestudygroups.com. Another way is seeking recommendations from community members. They can guide you based on your location, needs, and preferences.

Be Committed and Consistent

Your growth is not only dependent on the community you join. It depends on your commitment and consistency. It may take time to adjust to your new spiritual environment. Still, the more consistent you become, participating in activities and being open in your views and questions, the more comfortable and engaging you become. Over time, you may have to evaluate your growth and adjust accordingly. Trying another group that deals directly with your goal and provides better support where needed is perfectly okay.

Starting a Bible Study Group if None Is Available

It's quite interesting starting a Bible study group. However, it can be scary and intimidating. Think of it as like school when you had difficulty understanding a course and approached a classmate who understood better. It's not so different from a Bible study group, except you must be dedicated and committed to this noble cause. You are not alone. Jesus lived this life, and He will help you every step of the way. Here are things to consider as you plan your group:

- **Give Purpose to Your Meetings**. Find out what to achieve with each meeting. Plan the beginning with the end in mind. If there's a need you've noticed is lacking among believers, you can set that as a goal for your study group. Pray as you prepare so you know you're led by God. If you're led by God, rest assured He has a plan for your study group.

- **Seek Counsel and Set Up Meeting Times**. You can seek counsel and ask questions from spiritual mentors and friends. Afterward, set up a meeting time and communicate it with future group members. Arrange for the first meeting in your house, backyard, local bakery, or anywhere easily accessible by everyone. You cannot achieve this alone, so reach out to someone willing to assist. Ensure the time for the meetings is favorable for those attending.

- **Get Materials.** Gather materials to create a curriculum for your Bible study group and spread it across several months. It helps you be more intentional and focused. You can prepare, study, and pray for God's Spirit to control your meetings.

People usually open up and feel welcome in an environment they know is safe. So, creating a welcoming and respectful atmosphere where members can feel at ease is imperative. A welcoming environment helps members feel comfortable sharing questions, doubts, and insights without fear of judgment. A respectful conversation promotes active listening behavior and builds trust. Let these be the goals of your meetings, reflecting God's love, encouraging participation, promoting spiritual activities, creating unity among brethren, honoring God's presence, and dividing God's Word in truth to build spirits to overcome life challenges.

Roles and Responsibilities within a Bible Group

There are several responsibilities and roles within a community. You cannot fulfill every position, so delegating tasks encourages productivity and a meaningful experience. Here are key roles in a Bible study group:

Leader or Facilitator: A facilitator's role is to prepare and lead the discussions, introduce the topic, and ask questions related to the text. At the end of the study, they summarize the teaching and provide a lesson for members to take home and guidelines on applying those lessons in different scenarios. They keep the group focused on the topic, which helps the members manage conflicts and disruption. They encourage members to participate in discussions, ensuring everyone has an opportunity to share their take on the teachings and offer insights for a better understanding of the topic.

Group Members: They present themselves for group meetings and prepare ahead for each study by reading the assigned texts and materials. They listen respectfully to the leader and other members, engage in constructive dialogue, and ask questions to help them clarify the text.

Members can share how the scriptures apply to them.

Key Note Takers or Recorders: As much as the members are part of the meeting, they help the facilitator summarize the discussions, and if permitted, they provide a recorded study of the discussions. It becomes valuable for future references and helps the facilitator and members refer to those teachings when needed.

Prayer Groups: This is usually headed by the facilitator, but members can be a part of the prayer group. They lead the prayers before and after discussions, ushering God's presence into the meeting and interceding for the member's needs.

The scriptures often address these roles precisely. Acts 2:42, 46-47 says:

> *"All the believers devoted themselves to the apostles' teaching, and to fellowship, and to sharing in meals (including the Lord's Supper), and to prayer.... They worshiped together at the Temple each day, met in homes for the Lord's Supper, and shared their meals with great joy and generosity— all the while praising God and enjoying the goodwill of all the people. And each day the Lord added to their fellowship those who were being saved."*

More Tips on Effective Facilitation

Here are more tips to help you understand the role of a facilitator better:

- **Prepare for Your Audience.** You must always have the end goal in mind. Ask questions like, "What is this Bible study for?" and " Who is it for?" People understand and comprehend things differently, so your audience will determine your teaching approach. Prepare your study according to your audience's age group. If you have more teens, include more examples based on the lives of other teenagers.

- **Prepare to Share the Word in Context and Literature.** Know how cultural and historical context gives different interpretations of scriptures. You can prepare your teachings from this angle. Make it fun and rich in value.

- **Manage Questions and Opinions with Grace.** It's your virtues that separate you from everyone else. How you act in challenging situations, the fruit of the Spirit you exhibit in different issues, how you listen not to judge but to counsel, your patience toward members, and your excellence in delivering God's Word. These virtues are people's encounters with you. Do not ever think of yourself above other members. You must learn to make allowances for mistakes and errors.

Colossians 4:6 (KJV) says:

"Let your speech be always with grace, seasoned with salt, that ye may know how ye ought to answer every man."

Community fosters an opportunity for fellowship. One of God's sole aims for creating the church was fellowship with others. As you've seen through the scriptures, Christians dwelt together in love and unity, praying and praising as they were taught God's Word by the apostles. To add flavor to your meetings, you could invite guest speakers and allow members to share their perspectives of God's Word. Use resources and share them as short tasks and take-home assignments. Encourage breakout sessions and, most importantly, hold worship and praise sessions.

Conclusion

Take a moment to reflect on your journey. You've covered significant ground, from understanding the basics of Bible interpretation and applying its teachings to creating a consistent study routine, recognizing key Biblical themes, and appreciating the historical and cultural contexts that shape the scriptures.

You discovered the value of using study tools and resources and saw how studying the Bible within a community can bring diverse perspectives, mutual encouragement, and accountability. Each chapter promises to equip you with practical strategies to deepen your understanding of God's Word and strengthen your relationship with Him.

However, this book is more than a set of instructions. It's a companion on your spiritual journey, no matter where you started. Whether you are building a stronger faith, seeking answers to life's questions, or wanting to know God more intimately, this book aims to support and enlighten you every step of the way.

Sometimes, you feel like you're reading the Bible but not absorbing its message, or the words aren't sticking. You're not alone or out of line. There's a story about a little boy who once faced the same issue. He went to his grandfather and said, "Grandpa, I keep reading the Bible, but nothing seems to stay with me. I don't understand anything I'm reading."

His grandfather thought for a moment and then told the boy to take a coal bag and fill it with water from the river. The bag was full of holes from their mining days because they were a family of coal miners. The boy did as he was told, but the water had leaked out by the time he returned. The grandfather asked him to try again. The boy returned to the river, filled the bag, and hurried back, but the water was gone once more. The frustrated boy said, "There's no point. The water keeps leaking out."

The grandfather smiled and said, "Look at the bag. It may not hold water, but now it's cleaner. The same is true with God's Word. Even when you feel like you don't retain anything, God is working within you, cleansing and renewing your spirit."

Spiritual growth isn't visible, but that doesn't mean it isn't happening. God's Word is alive and active, working within you to cleanse and transform you, even when you think you're not progressing. Like the coal bag was rinsed clean, consistent study of the Bible fills you with the wisdom and knowledge God has in store for you.

As you study and meditate on the scriptures, trust that it leads you toward greater spiritual maturity. Like the mustard seed that grows into a large tree, your faith and understanding will bloom, offering shelter and hope to others.

Keep these lessons close to your heart. Let them guide your walk with God, knowing you are never alone on this journey. You'll watch your faith and understanding flourish, leading you to a deeper, more fulfilling relationship with the Lord with patience, perseverance, and a like-minded community's support.

Check out another book in the series

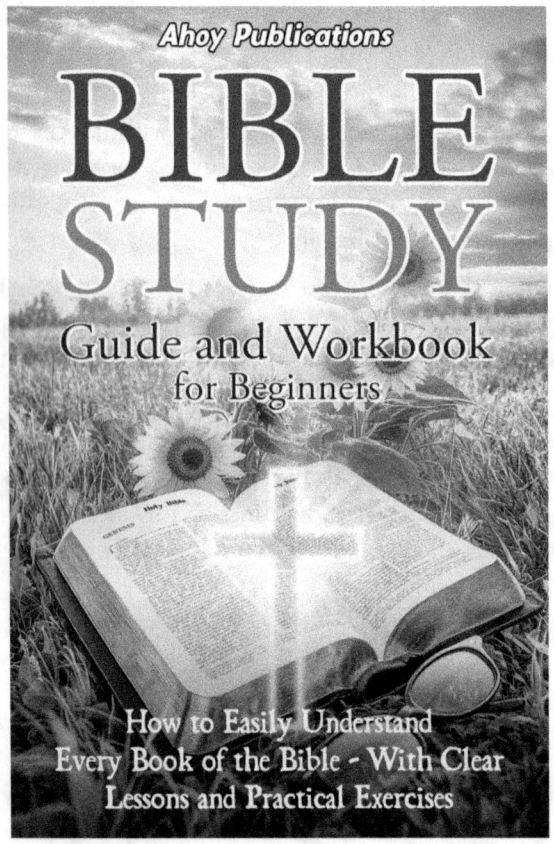

Welcome Aboard, Check Out This Limited-Time Free Bonus!

Ahoy, reader! Welcome to the Ahoy Publications family, and thanks for snagging a copy of this book! Since you've chosen to join us on this journey, we'd like to offer you something special.

Check out the link below for a FREE e-book filled with delightful facts about American History.

But that's not all - you'll also have access to our exclusive email list with even more free e-books and insider knowledge. Well, what are ye waiting for? Click the link below to join and set sail toward exciting adventures in American History.

Access your bonus here

https://ahoypublications.com/

Or, Scan the QR code!

References

5 Steps to Understanding Any Biblical Text: The Interpretive Journey.... (2015). Zondervan Academic. https://zondervanacademic.com/blog/5-steps-to-understanding-any-biblical-text

7 Benefits of Joining a Bible Study Group. (2024). The KJV Store. https://www.thekjvstore.com/articles/7-benefits-of-joining-a-bible-study-group/

7 Benefits of Joining a Bible Study Group – ClearView Baptist Church. (2024, March 6). Www.clearview.org. https://www.clearview.org/blog/christian-life/7-benefits-of-joining-a-bible-study-group/

A Guide to Finding the Right Bible Translation. (2021, June 10). Olive Tree Blog. https://www.olivetree.com/blog/a-guide-to-finding-the-right-bible-translation/

Adventist Team. (n.d.). Applying the Bible to Your Daily Life. Adventist.org. https://www.adventist.org/holy-scriptures/applying-bible-to-daily-life/

Armstrong, A. (2024, January 21). What are the best Bible study tools for beginners? Aaron Armstrong. https://aaronarmstrong.co/what-are-the-best-bible-study-tools-for-beginners/

Brown, G. (n.d.). Lesson 16: Major Bible Themes Of Scripture | Bible.org. Bible.org. https://bible.org/seriespage/lesson-16-major-bible-themes-scripture

Cater, C. (2023, May 24). How to Study Your Bible: 7 Basic Principles of Biblical Interpretation. Precept. https://www.precept.org/2023/05/7-basic-principles-of-biblical-interpretation/

CBMW. (2007, November 5). The New Testament Approach: Setting and Culture. CBMW. https://cbmw.org/2007/11/05/the-new-testament-approach-setting-and-culture/

Ch'ng, A. (2018, December 6). Accuracy, Readability, Usability: How We Chose Our Bible Translation. The Gospel Coalition | Australia. https://au.thegospelcoalition.org/article/accuracy-readability-usability-chose-bible-translation/

Cho, S. (2024, April). 10 most common themes you'll find in Biblical stories. Bible Scripture. https://biblescripture.net/10-most-common-themes-youll-find-in-biblical-stories/

Christian, V. (2023, August 30). Interpreting Words: How to Use a Bible Dictionary to Guide Your Understanding. Vera Christian. https://www.verachristian.com/connecting-the-dots/interpreting-words-bible-dictionary

D., V. (2023, July 7). Unpacking the 14 Most Powerful Themes in the Bible. Be in Not Of. https://beinnotof.com/post/biblethemes

Davis, D. (2023, May 24). 5 Resources to Understand the Historical Context of the Bible: A Guide for Meaningful Interpretation. Equipped Servant. https://www.equippedservant.com/blog/five-resources-to-understand-historical-context-bible

Davis, K. (2017, April 15). Understanding Different Types of Bible Translations. LIVING WATERS CHURCH. https://www.lwch.org/read/2017/4/7/understanding-the-different-types-of-bible-translations

DeRouchie, J. S. (2020, September 11). Interpreting Scripture: A General Introduction. The Gospel Coalition. https://www.thegospelcoalition.org/essay/interpreting-scripture-a-general-introduction/

Doerksen, R. (2022, January 6). MacGregor EMC. MacGregor EMC. https://www.macgregoremc.com/blog/a-guide-to-picking-bible-translations

Edwards, L. (2023, July 18). Trouble Being Consistent with Bible Study? Create a Bible Study Routine. Latoyaedwards.net. https://latoyaedwards.net/bible-study-routine/

FAQ: All These Bible Translations Confuse Me! (2023). Christian-History.org. https://www.christian-history.org/faq-bible-translations.html

Fisher, C. (2023, July 26). 10 Tips To Establish A Consistent Daily Bible Study Routine. Chadfisheronline.com; Mysite. https://www.chadfisheronline.com/post/10-tips-to-establish-a-consistent-daily-bible-study-routine

Five Steps of a Practical Bible Study. (2016). Questionsgod.com. https://www.questionsgod.com/bible-study-practical-method.htm

freebiblestudyhub.com. (2024, June 5). How to Find a Bible Study Group: A Comprehensive Guide. Medium; Medium.

ttps://medium.com/@phankimhien83/how-to-find-a-bible-study-group-a-comprehensive-guide-bbd3d8113065

Genres in the Bible. (n.d.). Www.intothyword.org.
http://www.intothyword.org/apps/articles/default.asp?articleid=31435

gnasim. (2023, October 15). A Comprehensive Guide to Effective Bible Study: Tools, Techniques, and Life Applications – Chmeetings. ChMeetings Church Management Software. https://www.chmeetings.com/a-comprehensive-guide-to-effective-bible-study-tools-techniques-and-life-applications/

Guest Writer. (2024, April 2). Five Ways to Be More Consistent with Your Bible Study Routine. Living by Design Ministries. https://livingbydesign.org/bible-study-routine-2/

Historical and Cultural Context – Todd Miles | Free Online Bible. (n.d.). Www.biblicaltraining.org. https://www.biblicaltraining.org/learn/academy/nt310-hermeneutics/nt310-11-historical-cultural-context

How Often Should I Study the Bible? (n.d.). Scripture Confident Living. https://www.scriptureconfidentliving.com/blog/how-often-should-i-study-the-bible

How should the different genres of the Bible impact how we interpret the Bible? (2022, April 12). GotQuestions.org. https://www.gotquestions.org/Bible-genres.html

How to choose a Bible translation. (2022, November 17). Wycliffe Bible Translators. https://wycliffe.org.uk/story/how-to-choose-the-best-bible-translation

HPG. (2022, March 23). 5 Tips to Choose a Bible Translation Right for You. Www.hendricksonrose.com. https://www.hendricksonrose.com/stories/5-tips-choose-bible-translation-right-you

INTRODUCTION TO PRINCIPLES OF BIBLE INTERPRETATION WHY STUDY THIS? We Must Know How to Understand and Teach the Bible Properly. (n.d.). https://www.mbcmi.org/wp-content/uploads/2018/06/Principles-of-Bible-Interpretation.pdf

Kathy. (2024, March 4). 4 Tips for Handling Difficult Bible Passages – Kathy Howard. Kathy Howard. https://www.kathyhoward.org/4-tips-for-handling-difficult-bible-passages/

katrinadhamel. (2020, February 20). The Importance of Culture and History in Bible Study. Katrina D Hamel. https://www.katrinadhamel.com/post/the-importance-of-culture-and-history-in-bible-study

Kight, C. (n.d.). 14 Reasons to Read the Bible | Cru. Cru.org. https://www.cru.org/us/en/train-and-grow/bible-studies/reasons-read-bible.html

Lesson 6: Principles of Biblical Interpretation | Bible.org. (n.d.). Bible.org. https://bible.org/seriespage/lesson-6-principles-biblical-interpretation

Love in the Bible | Resource Guide | BibleProjectTM. (2022, December 15). BibleProject. https://bibleproject.com/guides/love-in-the-bible/

Martin, L. R. (2018, June 5). Biblical Commands and Cultural Context. Evangel Magazine. https://www.evangelmagazine.com/2018/06/biblical-commands-and-cultural-context/

McDill, W. (2014, March 12). 7 Principles of Biblical Interpretation. Lifeway Research. https://research.lifeway.com/2014/03/12/7-principles-of-biblical-interpretation/

NRJohnson. (2013, November 15). The Importance and Benefits of Bible Study – Deeper Christian. Deeperchristian.com. https://deeperchristian.com/bible-study-benefits-samuel-brengle/

Perry, D. W. (2010, February 1). Christ and Culture in the Old Testament. Www.churchofjesuschrist.org. https://www.churchofjesuschrist.org/study/ensign/2010/02/christ-and-culture-in-the-old-testament?lang=eng

Porter, T. (2019, December 16). How To Start a Group Bible Study – Terry Porter. Terry Porter. https://terry-porter.com/how-to-start-a-group-bible-study/

Remkiv, T. (2023, July 3). 4 Reasons Historical and Cultural Context in the Bible Matters. Tanyaremkiv. https://tanyaremkiv.com/2023/07/03/4-reasons-historical-and-cultural-context-in-the-bible-matters/

Staff, L. (2023, June 19). 29 Bible Study Tools for Reading the Bible More Effectively. Word by Word. https://www.logos.com/grow/bible-study-tools/?srsltid=AfmBOoq-NC-ZB0i-ZaxCIWUQ7uEe4OG3chfaE5FpRuxHww-k39ltmuBO

The Best Bible Study Tools For Deeper…. (n.d.). Love Worth Finding Ministries. https://www.lwf.org/ultimate-guide-to-bible-study/best-bible-study-tools-for-deeper-understanding

Topical Study: How to Study Themes in Scripture – Bible Study Tips. (2024). Bible Study Tips. https://biblestudy.tips/topical-study/

University, G. (2023, June 1). Navigating the Different Bible Versions: A Guide for Christian Education. Global University. https://globaluniversity.edu/navigating-different-bible-versions-a-guide-for-christian-education/

What is Application? – Olive Tree Blog. (2024, July 29). Olivetree.com. https://www.olivetree.com/blog/what-is-application/

Image Sources

[1] https://unsplash.com/photos/boy-reading-holy-bible-while-lying-on-bed-NaWKMlp3tVs

[2] *Designed by Freepik,* https://www.freepik.com/free-photo/rear-view-young-woman-with-open-arms-meadow_931397.htm

[3] https://unsplash.com/photos/person-writing-on-white-paper-YnRNdB-XTME

[4] https://unsplash.com/photos/three-the-holy-bibles-NVnIyjv0_wQ

[5] https://unsplash.com/photos/person-reading-book-G-_L3Egkqmc

[6] https://unsplash.com/photos/person-holding-bible-with-pen-oUiTrFhnEkE

[7] https://unsplash.com/photos/white-printer-paper-with-kanji-text-CEbyMSUu1mg

[8] https://unsplash.com/photos/beige-page-of-book-eaU0tA0xTxI

[9] *stained glass: Alfred Handel, photograph:Toby Hudson, CC BY-SA 3.0* <https://creativecommons.org/licenses/by-sa/3.0>*, via Wikimedia Commons* https://commons.wikimedia.org/wiki/File:StJohnsAshfield_StainedGlass_GoodShepherd-frame_crop.jpg

[10] *Daderot, CC0, via Wikimedia Commons* https://commons.wikimedia.org/wiki/File:Epistles_of_Saint_Peter,_Single_Leaf_from_a_Manuscript_Psalter_and_New_Testament,_about_1084,_Byzantium,_Constantinople,_ink,_tempera,_and_gold_on_vellum_-_Cleveland_Museum_of_Art_-_DSC08417.JPG

[11] https://unsplash.com/photos/man-in-black-long-sleeve-shirt-writing-on-white-paper-QiLPQeQSXD0

[12] https://unsplash.com/photos/silver-macbook-pro-3iT3dnmblGE

[13] https://unsplash.com/photos/landscape-shot-of-white-cross-during-daytime-ia0Zxx_sDr8

[14] https://www.pexels.com/photo/sculpture-of-julius-caesar-18088652/

[15] https://www.pexels.com/photo/ancient-egyptian-statues-outside-hatshepsut-temple-deir-el-bahari-egypt-5572512/

[16] Abraham Bosse, CC0, via Wikimedia Commons
https://commons.wikimedia.org/wiki/File:David_with_the_Head_of_Goliath_MET_DP818740.jpg

[17] https://www.pexels.com/photo/people-reading-and-studying-the-bible-13011294/

[18] https://www.pexels.com/photo/a-grayscale-of-a-lady-justice-figurine-6077181/

[19] https://unsplash.com/photos/man-in-black-suit-jacket-sitting-on-chair-n9H1UuYj-cg

[20] https://unsplash.com/photos/woman-sitting-on-brown-bench-while-reading-book-vtCBruWoNqo

[21] https://unsplash.com/photos/four-women-looking-down-rTwhmFSoXC8

www.ingramcontent.com/pod-product-compliance
Lightning Source LLC
Chambersburg PA
CBHW071531120626
46550CB00006B/2417